Principles and Practices of Oral Communication

Appraisal Theory and Its Application to Casual Conversation

Dr Sook Hee Lee

(MEd in Educational Psychology; MEd in TESOL; PhD in TESOL)

A catalogue record for this book is available from the British Library

ISBN: 978-1-907962-94-3

Published by Cranmore Publications

www.cranmorepublications.co.uk

Praise for *Principles and Practices of Oral Communication*

This is a quirky, interesting, playful book that provides a very **interesting and distinctive** approach to understanding how the English language can be used to evaluate our experiences, the people we meet and the things and phenomena we encounter. It expresses the **exceptional talent that Dr Susan Lee has** for introducing **her passion for systemic functional linguistics** into very **practical, very amusing** language learning activities for those learning English as a second or foreign language – and also for speakers of English learning more about how we evaluate based on our feelings, our judgements of truthfulness and morality and our appreciation of events, performances, creations and natural phenomena. *Principles and Practices of Oral Communication* shows how a powerful linguistic theory can be used to produce **effective and enjoyable** language learning experiences. This is an important book by a truly scholarly teacher who has drawn on her own experience as an English language learner to empower all who read this work.

Dr Len Unsworth

Professor in English and Literacies Education
Australian Catholic University, Sydney

This book embodies a **unique** approach to describing aspects of the English language which learners often do not get taught but which are essential to function effectively in an English-speaking environment. The application of the appraisal model of evaluative language in resources for language learners **is novel**, and the focus on words ending in –y allows **a surprisingly wide range of commonly-used evaluative** terms to be introduced and exemplified.

Professor Geoff Thompson

Honorary Senior Fellow, School of English, University of Liverpool, UK

Visiting Professor, Sun Yat-sen University, Guangzhou

Guest Professor, University of Science and Technology, Beijing

This book will be **very useful for teachers and learners alike**. The author has identified a very interesting area of language that will make users sound more natural and takes their vocabulary to places most **coursebooks have previously ignored**.

Richard Pincus

Head of teaching at the Embassy Language Centre, Sydney, Australia

This book is well written and fun to read. I strongly recommend it to those who want to develop a **critical ability** in English speaking and writing.

Dr Xinghua Liu

PhD (Reading, UK)

Lecturer of Applied Linguistics, Shanghai Jiao Tong University, China

Principles and Practices of Oral Communication is **really interesting** and provides **essential and crucial** knowledge for those who are studying English.

Haneul Lee

An international university student from South Korea

TABLE OF CONTENTS

Acknowledgements

With the deepest gratitude firstly I wish to thank God for guiding me through constant inspiration and personal revelation. I also deeply express my gratitude to the following people for their magnificent support and contribution to the production of this book.

Gratitude goes to the Embassy teachers, including the Director Carolyn Matthews who generously allowed me to conduct a survey with willing cooperation. In particular, special thanks should be given to the Embassy teachers Richard Pincus, Antoine Burke, Dominic Chellet, Angelika Maag and Jenny Barreiros for sharing their ideas and for reading through the draft and providing valuable feedback.

I would like to thank my PhD supervisor Professor Len Unsworth for providing a terrific book review despite his extremely busy schedule. I am most grateful to Professor Geoff Thompson for providing insightful comments and a wonderful book review. Thanks to the following SFL scholars for their encouragement and support on my scholarly journey: Professor Jim Martin, Dr Peter White, Dr Sally Humphrey, Dr Susan Hood, Dr David Rose and Helen Drury.

I acknowledge my lovely students and friendly colleagues at Charles Sturt University Sydney, and also my supervisor Dr Jeff Gosper and Director Sue Bakir for their support and for allowing me to use all the resources that were required for getting this book to the publication stage.

I appreciate the magnificent people who always generously proofread for me: John Magin, who is a teacher at Lloyd College, and Tiger Wise, an editor as well as In Wha Kim, who helped to design the cover.

I am also grateful to my PhD friend Dr Xinghua Liu who introduced me to my publisher and also to the team at Cranmore Publications who were interested in and dedicated to publishing my book.

And finally to my daughters, Mee-Jin Lee, Mee-Eun Lee and son Jong-do Lee, who illuminate every breath I take through their very existence, and to my husband Dr Il Kyu Lee for his support and trust in me.

✎ Test yourself!
Commonly used words that end in 'Y'

Please read through the following expressions containing commonly used words that end in 'Y' to see how many you know and use in everyday conversation. Simply tick the relevant column. If you tick less than 10 boxes in Column 1 then you need to consider buying this book.

	Column 1	Column 2	Column 3
	I know and use it in everyday conversation	I understand but I never use it	I don't know the expression
She is a very **bossy** woman.			
My neighbour tends to be **snobby.** They do not like to mix with people from other backgrounds.			
My 5-year-old boy is very **fussy.** He does not eat any vegetables.			
My husband is a very **finicky** person, while I am quite **laidback.**			
He's got a **quirky** sense of humour. Not everyone finds his jokes funny.			
Children usually get very **cranky** when they are not fed.			
He is very **grumpy** today for some reason.			
She is very **stingy.** She only gave me a card for my birthday.			
He is such a **jolly** guy.			
That mechanic is pretty **dodgy.**			
She is very **nasty.** So everyone hates her.			
He looks so **geeky** with those thick glasses he wears.			
There are all these **brainy** people at university.			
She usually wears **tacky** clothes.			
When the alarm bell rings, don't get all **panicky.**			
There are some pretty **freaky** people on Oxford Street on a Saturday night.			
It is very **fiddly** to make this kind of jewellery. You need very steady hands.			
Total			

How many boxes did you tick in Column 1?

1-5 (　)　　　6-10 (　)　　　11-15 (　)　　　More than 15 (　)

I. Why this book is valuable

This book explains key principles involved in teaching oral communication and outlines how they can be utilized to learn the casual conversation that is used in everyday life situations. The principle side of the theoretical framework used in the book arises out of my PhD research which was conducted at the University of Sydney.

The practical side of the book arises from my experience of living in Australia for 20 years and tutoring students at Charles Sturt University in Sydney, and numerous EAP (English for Academic Purposes) as well as IELTS (International English Language Testing System) courses in colleges in Sydney over the past 7 years. Throughout my almost 20 years of living in Australia, I have noticed that native English speakers like Aussies (referring to Australians) hate using long expressions and love to abbreviate them into short phrases by placing Y at the end (e.g. fussy, bossy, freaky, finicky, cranky, etc.). An example is 'bossy' which is from the word 'a boss' and is used when someone's behaviour is authoritative or overbearing. Other examples, albeit from different roots, include breakfast-brekky, television-telly, football-footy. That is, there seems to be a big gap between the English that I learned in my country and what is apparent in Australia.

My assumption regarding this gap was proven when I conducted a preliminary survey on the use of expressions ending in 'Y'. The participants were ESL (English as Second Language) students studying English at an English Language Centre in Sydney. The Language Centre is located in the same building as the Charles Sturt University Study Centre in Sydney where I teach academic writing courses. A survey consisting of expressions was used for the assessment (see the previous section). After permission from the Director of the Language Centre, I approached English teachers to have them administer the assessment.

A total of 74 students from 6 different levels of English classes participated in the survey. The English classes were EAP 1 (8), II (9), III (11), Advanced (8), Upper Intermediate I (10), and II (11). While their length of stay in Australia varied, the average was approximately 4 months. The majority of the students were from Vietnam, South Korea, China and Colombia.

Average of the students' knowledge of Y ending expressions

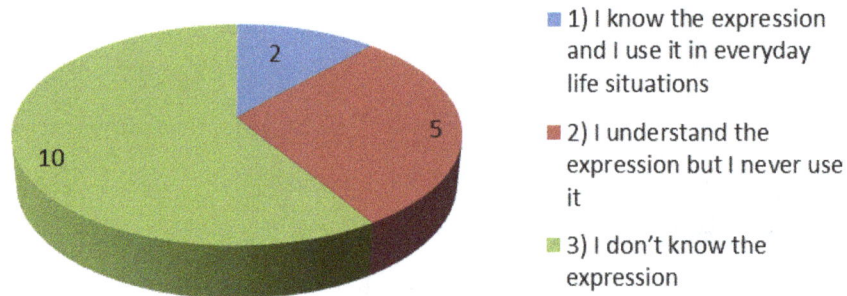

- ■ 1) I know the expression and I use it in everyday life situations
- ■ 2) I understand the expression but I never use it
- ■ 3) I don't know the expression

The students were required to rate 17 examples of evaluative words ending in 'Y' in accordance with three levels of its usage (see the Pie Chart above). The results of the survey revealed that **the students knew and used only 2 expressions out of 17 on average** (Category 1). Category 2 represents the gap between linguistic competence and performance. On average, the students scored 5 out of 17. When it comes to Category 3 the average student score was 10 out of 17. This means that most ESL students do not know these expressions at all. When combining categories 2 and 3 (5 + 10 = 15), we need to conclude that this book is **very useful as the students barely knew the expressions.**

There seems to be little link between the length of stay in an English-speaking country and the level of knowledge of these expressions. The results clearly demonstrate that the vast majority of ESL students are not familiar with Y ending evaluative language, irrespective of how long they have lived in an English speaking country. I assume that this phenomenon will occur across all levels of ESL learners regardless of their existing knowledge of English.

II. About the author

My unique background and the circumstances in which I learnt English have motivated me to produce the practice side of my book. I myself am from an ESL background, having learned English from scratch and have since become an English teacher at a university in Australia. I was born in South Korea but have lived in Australia for almost 20 years. In South Korea, I obtained a Bachelor's degree in Chemistry Education, co-majoring in English literature, and then a Master's degree in Educational Psychology. Although English was not my major, I had a strong passion for it. My deep interest in learning English enabled me to attain a high standard of English grammar with an extensive vocabulary range. Despite that, like many EFL (English as a Foreign Language) learners, when I first arrived in Sydney Australia in 1991 at the age of 35, I could barely speak a word of English. I accompanied my husband who intended to pursue his PhD in Computer Science at the University of Wollongong in N.S.W., Australia. Wollongong is a small city, about two hours drive from Sydney. I had three little children. Due to the stress caused both by financial constraints and my inability to express myself, I contracted Lymphoid Tuberculosis. I thought I was going to die when I was diagnosed with the disease and subsequently underwent two major operations. I took a variety of medications for one and half years every day until I finally recovered from the illness.

My intensive English learning was made possible when I was granted PR (permanent residency) from the Australian government in 1995. I enrolled in an English preparation course for six months to learn how to speak English but my speaking ability was still unsatisfactory. This led me to enrol in a Master's course in TESOL (Teaching of English to Speakers of Other Languages) at the University of Wollongong in the hope of improving my speaking skills. It was during this course that I was exposed to Systemic Functional Linguistics (SFL) theory. I was so fascinated by the theory because the Functional Grammar approach was very different from the traditional grammar and cognitive process approaches through which we learned English back in my country. SFL theory was formulated by M.A.K. Halliday, one of the most prominent scholars in the field of linguistics. He currently holds an honorary position in the Linguistics Department at the University of Sydney. The theory is based on a socio-linguistic orientation in contrast to

Chomsky's psycho-linguistic orientation. After I completed my Masters in TESOL at the University of Wollongong in 2000, I was offered a scholarship at the University of Sydney to do a PhD degree in TESOL.

My PhD was about writing academic essays critically from a linguistic perspective. During this period, a new theory called 'Appraisal', which is concerned with evaluative language, was developed from interpersonal meaning within a SFL framework (see details in Sections 1 and 2). Based on Halliday's (1994) broad notion of interpersonal resources such as speech functions, modality, and attitudinal lexis, the appraisal theory has been further refined by his followers such as Jim Martin and Peter White, who were involved in the Write it Right project sponsored by the NSW Department of Education (Write it Right, 1996). That is, appraisal theory is an extension and a further refinement of existing interpersonal resources. The theory has been initially developed in the contexts of history studies and mass media studies mostly at high schools in NSW (see details, Macken-Horarik & Martin, 2003; Martin & White, 2005/2007; Martin & Rose, 2003/2007, Hood, 2006; 2010; White, 1998, 2004).

My PhD was basically about applying this new theory in an academic writing context in order to address university students' lack of critical voice in their writing. As a result of this, the theory has been extended a great deal to accommodate it in academic writing. As far as I know, I was the first scholar from South Korea who completed a PhD using the SFL framework and I am one of the few scholars who have used the Appraisal system in academic writing. After completing my PhD in 2005, I have published 9 papers by myself in internationally renowned journals and a book relating to academic writing (see the reference list at the back). I now have a substantial amount of expertise in the field of academic literacy. The ideas and philosophies underpinning the theoretical frameworks used in this book are drawn from the SFL and Appraisal theories used in my PhD. After my PhD, I taught IELTS and EAP courses at several colleges. I am currently employed by Study Group Australia as the Study Support Coordinator for students enrolled at the Charles Sturt University Study Centre in Sydney and am an adjunct lecturer at the university. My main role is to teach how to write academic essays to both local Australian students and international students from 60 nationalities both at undergraduate and postgraduate level. I am a reviewer of the Journal of US-China Foreign Language and Sino-US English Teaching and am on the Editorial Board of the TESOL Journal, a sister journal to the Asian EFL Journal. I am also a member of the Association for Academic Language and Learning (AALL) and the Australian Systemic Functional Linguistics Association (ASFLA). I am a regular columnist in the Korean Top Weekly Newspaper, which has been published in Sydney since 2008.

III. Why this book is unique

I believe that this book will be extremely useful for those who are involved in teaching English as an additional language as well as for ESL/EFL students. This is because there are several features that distinguish this book from other casual conversation teaching materials.

✓ Firstly, in order to explain basic principles that govern oral communication, this book takes one of the models derived from the **Systemic Functional Linguistics (SFL)** approach, the **'appraisal'** theory (see details in Section 2). The theory is used as a framework for examining the use of evaluative words in casual conversation. One of the primary tenets of the SFL approach is that context is critical when examining the use of language. In this book, the context is casual conversation in Australian English. However, I am sure that most expressions are universally used in English-speaking countries such as America, the UK, Canada and New Zealand. The focus of this book is to put the appraisal system into practice by theorizing the casual conversation that is used in everyday life situations. As far as I know, no other book has used the theory to explain how oral communication works.

✓ Secondly, in this book I collate adjectival expressions that end in/with 'Y'. While I was living in Wollongong for 8 years, I had many opportunities to meet local Australians. During this time I was exposed to the expressions that ordinary native English speakers use in everyday life situations. I have been compiling these expressions for almost 20 years.

✓ Thirdly, what is common among the 'Y' expressions chosen here is that they are all part of the evaluative language of the **ATTITUDE** system which is part of the Appraisal theory. Appraisal consists of basically three main features termed ATTITUDE, ENGAGEMENT and GRADUATION (see details in Section 2). To put it simply, one of the main reasons why people use language is to express their subjective opinions and views about things and people. This involves **evaluating things** positively or negatively (e.g. Sydney is beautiful, this room is messy), **evaluating people's behavior** (he is kind, she is a liar), and **expressing emotions and feelings** (I feel happy, I feel tired). This expression is called **ATTITUDE**. I realised that the Y ending evaluations can fit neatly into the ATTITUDE system. This book focuses on the ATTITUDE system.

There are two main reasons why it is very important to compile a list of evaluative language ending in Y using the **ATTITUDE system**. Firstly, the expressions sound simple and easy in English but when they are translated into the students' native languages, these expressions become lengthy and complicated. Secondly, as my PhD results reveal and teachers of English acknowledge, learners find it difficult to develop their critical stance in relation to others. This is because ESL/EFL learners, in particular from Asian backgrounds, are from so called 'Communication Reticent Cultures' where expressing their opinions or views is suppressed to some degree. The Y expressions will enable them to articulate their attitude succinctly and confidently in an appropriate context. From a teacher perspective, the ATTITUDE system will assist teachers to understand such issues as identity, subjectivity, positioning, voice, stance, etc. in the communication.

This collection of evaluative language will also help students to keep abreast of the recent emphasis on the importance of having 'emotional intelligence' and "I feel statements" (Burns, 2008, p.134) which are thought to be necessary for successful communication in any relationship.

✓ Fourthly, this book also covers many other similar collocations of Y endings that can be usefully employed in slightly different contexts. This means that students will be able to learn additional synonyms that are used by native English speakers for effective communication. The examples of Y ending expressions and other relevant expressions provided here have been gathered from various sources to reflect both current and historical usage. I have included as many authentic or relevant uses of the language as possible.

✓ Finally, the book also includes grammar exercises in areas where, based on my teaching experience, many ESL/EFL learners are most prone to making errors. Learning '**speech grammar**' is important, as it is an effective approach for general language proficiency (Donaldson, 2011). The speech grammar, of course, can be transferable to the grammar required in writing. Learners will find it much easier to communicate with native English speakers once they have mastered the expressions ending with 'Y', together with other expressions and grammar pertaining to the 'Y' evaluative language. While this book deals with a survival level of spoken English, learners will notice that their writing skills will also have improved significantly.

IV. Why I devoted myself to writing this book

There are three main factors that have motivated me to write this book.

- ✓ Firstly, I wanted to introduce SFL theory and to demonstrate how it applies to oral communication in a casual conversation context. I have noticed that since teaching English has become so popular and demanding, many native English-speaking people tend to be involved in teaching English without being appropriately equipped with theory. Previous studies have well documented that Australian teachers are anxious about their limited knowledge in language teaching. Furthermore, they are uncertain about what is an appropriate pedagogy for teaching language. Their anxiety stems mainly from the fact that there are few models available (Hammond & Macken-Horarik, 2001; Jones & Chen, 2012). It is assumed that this anxiety may exist in most English teachers working in other countries as well.

I believe that it is important for an English teacher to be equipped with a theory when they are involved in teaching a language. While I assume that language teachers understand other theories, I believe that not too many teachers have been exposed to the SFL theory. The most popular theories that underlie casual conversation books are notional-functional approaches and task-based approaches where situational context is emphasised. What characterises SFL theory is that while context plays a key role in meaning-making, meaning/function is a starting point and grammar is attached to the meaning. That is, contexts, meaning (semantics) and grammar (syntactic) are systematically linked to one another. SFL theory helps us to understand, above all, why the language is as it is and thus provides reasons why we make the linguistic choice that we do. Therefore, learning English is guided by both theory and meaning, unlike in the past. English learning becomes immediately meaningful and functional in a systematic way.

✓ Secondly, I wanted to introduce the appraisal theory and demonstrate how it can be used to address the issue of effective communication. Within SFL, this book uses the appraisal theory as a framework to teach the English language. There are some textbooks currently on the market that cover evaluative language. Therefore, this book is not something new with regards to this. However, unlike the existing conversation books published so far, all these evaluative expressions are organized based on the rigorous framework of the 'Appraisal system' formulated within Systemic Functional Linguistics (SFL) theory. The appraisal theory has come to be highly regarded in Australia and England. Some American scholars have also begun to show interest in the theory.

While SFL theory provides a very comprehensive and integrative framework, some reservations from language teachers have been expressed because of their difficulty in understanding the metalanguage used and its application to real teaching. In my PhD, built upon these scholars' innovative and dedicated work, I have expanded this theory in an academic discourse and I have developed a teaching framework called '**interpersonal meaning drive pedagogy**' (IMDP) to teach academic writing to university students (see details, Lee, 2006, 2008a, 2008b, 2010c, 2014). The IMPD model is basically derived from the appraisal theory, but other social approaches such as 'interaction in writing' from England, critical literacy and dialogic literacy have been also incorporated. This book is an aspect of the IMPD model that allows teachers to teach language from a social/interpersonal/dialogic perspective. The pedagogical approach used here is **newly developed and yet it is very simple, pragmatic, and comprehensive. This means that teachers can easily understand it without any prior knowledge of language teaching if they are willing to take some time digesting it**. My humble wish is that at the end of the day, this book will help to motivate students to learn English in an enjoyable way, while also providing knowledge of underlying theory.

✓ Thirdly, I feel that I have a compelling message to convey through this book and that my unique background enables me to be a 'gap filler'. As I said earlier, I have been an English learner for 20 years and a teacher for 7 years. I learned English throughout my 10 years schooling in South Korea, but I did not learn spoken English. After arriving in Australia, I spent another 10 years leaning to speak English. Since then I have been teaching English for 7 years. This unique background allowed me to notice a gap between the original culture and the target culture that has impacted on the ways of communication. There are big gaps between learners' existing knowledge and the new requirements. That is, there is a gap between Western audience expectations and students' real abilities to cope with communication when students make transitions.

It sounds presumptuous to say this, but native English teachers may have little idea of the gap between what the students have learned concerning English in their own countries and the unfamiliar expressions learners encounter in target countries. Teachers may easily take Y ending expressions for granted. Despite my deep knowledge of English vocabulary, I did not know real colloquial English such as the expressions ending in Y. Most students wish to learn English quickly and efficiently, given time and financial constraints. The importance of effective oral communication skills is equally important for university students because it greatly enhances their employability (Jones & Polly, 2013). This book is designed to bridge the gap.

While this book cannot be a panacea for mastering English, it will certainly provide a missing link between ESL/EFL learners' oral proficiency and the real English that is required to survive in English-speaking countries. Now ESL/EFL learners will be motivated to learn English not just in a rote-learning manner. English conversation skills can thus be acquired in an effective and enjoyable manner.

V. Target audience

This book targets a number of audiences.

- ✓ ESL/EFL teachers: English teachers are the primary audience for this book. The book will be a useful and cost effective teaching material for English teachers teaching both in an ESL/'inner circle mutilingual' and EFL/'expanding circle monolingual' context.

- ✓ TESOL/ELICOS teachers: Native English speaking teachers working at ELICOS (English Language Intensive Course for Overseas Students) colleges and those working in TESOL (Teaching English of other Speakers of Language) will benefit from the book.

- ✓ Any person who is interested in teaching English and non-English languages: Anyone who would like to be involved in teaching a language will also benefit from learning newly developed theories that explicate casual conversation. This book begins by introducing SFL approaches and, in particular, the newly-formulated appraisal theory. Even though the approaches are introduced in a casual conversation context, the frameworks can be applied in any context of language teaching.

- ✓ Adult students: I have written a companion book which is aimed at students (details can be found in the *More Information* section at the end of the book); however, students who are particularly interested in language theory will also find this book to be of value.

- ✓ Any person who is involved in interpersonal communication, such as counsellors and facilitators. The appraisal model is an extremely useful tool for understanding the nature of communication from a linguistic perspective.

VI. Section overview

This book consists of four sections:

- ✓ *Section 1* introduces SFL theory briefly from a broad perspective. The section also describes interpersonal meaning and how the 'Appraisal' system has been developed from it.

- ✓ *Section 2* focuses on explaining the 'ATTITUDE' system in detail, as it is a core and focal framework of the Appraisal theory that underpins the book. I have tried my best to use plain English to explain the theories. However, if you are not interested in understanding theoretical frameworks, you can skip Sections 1 and 2. I hope readers do not feel intimidated by the theories.

  When it comes to applying ATTITUDE into real teaching, teachers can simplify the system. They can ignore the terminology and simply use the expressions for emotions and for judging things/human behavior. They can use such words as positive versus negative evaluations depending on the level of the students. Based on my teaching experience, even EAP students can easily understand the simplified version of the framework when it comes to teaching how to raise critical voice.

- ✓ *Section 3* demonstrates the application of these theories to casual conversation on the basis of these frameworks.

- ✓ *Section 4* compiles other types of collocations and abbreviations pertaining to the group of expressions ending in Y.

Section 1: Key principles and approaches

1.1. The SFL approach

Systemic Functional Linguistics (SFL) is a useful way of explaining how oral as well as written communication function, categorizing all elements of a language. This is because the theory provides a comprehensive model that takes into account context, meaning or function (semantic) and grammar (syntactic) in a systemic way. What exactly is the SFL theory? As implied by its name, the SFL approach to language teaching is distinctively different compared to other approaches in three main ways.

Firstly, being **'functional'** means that function or meaning comes first and grammar is attached to the function. This is different from the traditional grammar approach where grammar is detached from its meaning. Most ESL/EFL students have learned under the traditional grammar approach with its psycholinguistics focus.

According to SFL theory, language is a resource for making meaning called a social semiotic (see details, Halliday & Matthiessen, 2004; Eggins, 2000; Butt et al., 2000; Thompson, 2013). This means that there are many ways of conveying a message to others such as body language, signs and symbols etc. However, using language is considered to be the most powerful means of communication. This also implies that people use language in order to make meanings with each other in their everyday social interactions. In this regards, SFL approaches are derived from sociolinguistics, as opposed to psycholinguistics, where writers/speakers' individual expressions are more highly regarded than the audience's reactions.

In SFL, the (English) language has evolved to serve three main functions of meaning simultaneously: **ideational** or experiential, **interpersonal** and **textual** functions. Under ideational function/meaning, we use language to share our experience of the world and this is Halliday's term for the ideas, content, and subject matter conveyed by language. Under the interpersonal function, we use language for interacting with others and expressing self and taking up positions to influence others. Textual function is concerned with information flow, making the meanings hang together within the language (see Figure 2).

'**Systemic**' conveys the notion that meaning is systematically interdependent on social context as well as on grammar. That is, meanings can be made not only by a correct use of grammar but also within appropriate contexts. This is different from process approaches, where psycho-linguistics is the basis. Under these approaches, pattern drills and practices are considered to be an important pedagogy. SFL theory stresses the importance of contexts that have an impact on the creation of meaningful text.

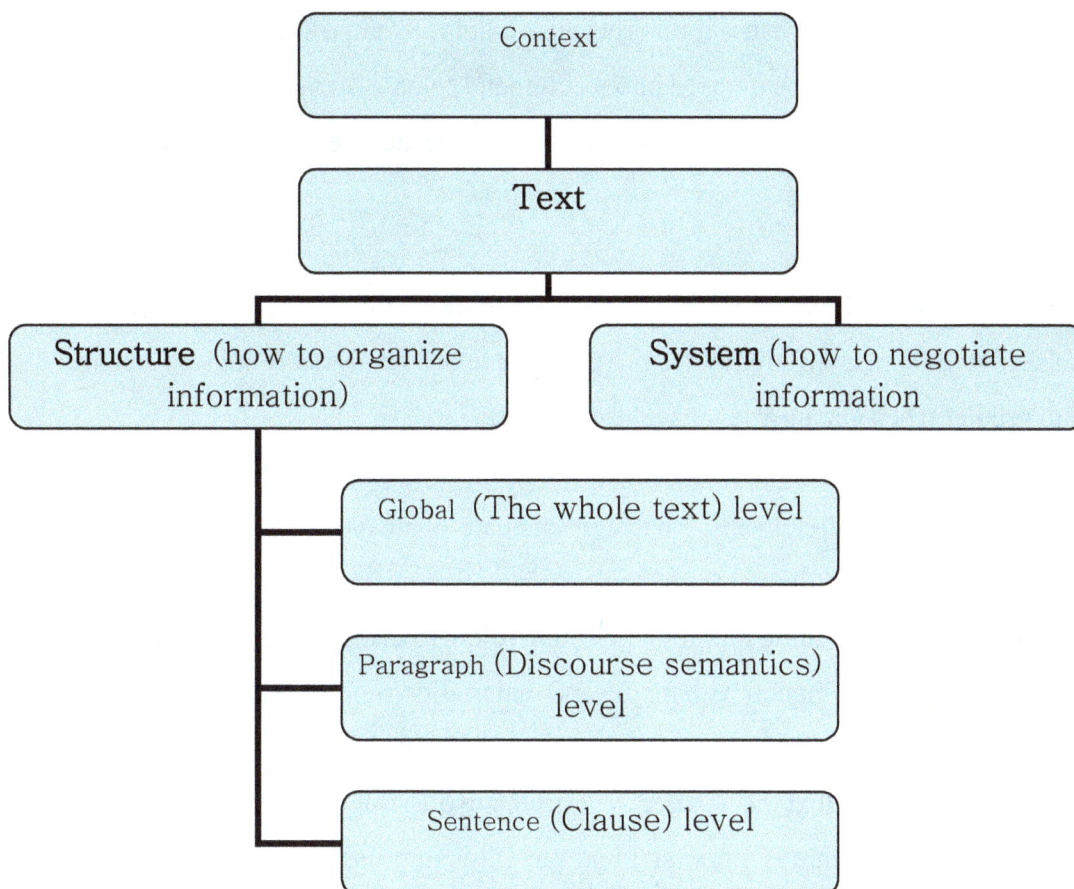

Figure 1: Text, structure and system from an interpersonal perspective

Under SFL, it is very important to understand the concept of 'text' before explaining the systematic links between context and text. A text refers to a complete linguistic interaction (spoken or written), preferably from beginning to end (Eggins, 2000). It is a piece of language in use. For example, this piece of language in use might be a greeting, an insult yelled from a car, or an email to a colleague. That is language that is functional (Butt et al., 2000). Text can be analysed by two broad aspects: 'structure' and (language) 'system' (see Figure 1). From an interpersonal perspective, while 'structure' refers to how to arrange/organize information according to the conventions and norms of the culture, 'system' refers to how to negotiate information. The structure can be analysed along three ranks: global (text), paragraph (discourse semantic) and sentence (clause). When we negotiate information, what we do is that we use persuasive expressions to receive assent while we send our message. For instance, in a sentence, it is important for international students to learn how to write a report, because it helps to empower them in their lives and work. The sentence can be phrased into a command 'please learn to write a report'. When sending this message, a writer utilises justifications (because, enables, empower) to create persuasion.

Now when we read text, we can deduce context from the text. For example, an SMS message will be read differently from a personal letter. Analysis of context can also help us to predict when and how language use will vary.

Contexts consist of 2 elements. Firstly, immediate contexts, termed '**register**', such as subject matter (field), the nature of the audience (tenor) and the channel which can be spoken or written including multimodality that refers to the mixture of textual, audio, and visual modes in combination with media and materiality (mode) (see Figure 2). Secondly, context is a broad cultural context termed '**genre**'. Genre is mostly relevant to the social purpose (Why) of the text that is directly reflected in the structure of the text. According to Martin (1984: 25), genre is more than text type. It is referred to as a set of "staged, goal-oriented social processes". Genre in general imposes constraints at the whole-text level of structure and relations, while register has an impact on language system at the level of the lexico-grammar of language features.

```
                    ┌──────────────────────┐
                    │  Context of Culture  │
                    │       (Genre)        │
                    │    and Situations    │
                    │     (Register:       │
                    │  Field, Tenor, Mode) │
                    │   (Power/Contact)    │
                    └──────────────────────┘

   ┌──────────────┐    ┌──────────────┐    ┌──────────────┐
   │  Ideational  │    │ Interpersonal│    │   Textual    │
   │Meaning/Function│   │              │    │              │
   └──────────────┘    └──────────────┘    └──────────────┘

              ┌──────────────┐    ┌──────────────┐
              │  Interaction │    │  Evaluation  │
              │(Speech functions)│ │  (Appraisal) │
              └──────────────┘    └──────────────┘

              ┌──────────────┐    ┌──────────────┐
              │ Mood system  │    │Evaluative language/│
              │ (Grammar) and│    │Appraisal system and│
              │ structure at │    │   structure  │
              │ discourse and│    │              │
              │ sentence level│   │              │
              └──────────────┘    └──────────────┘
```

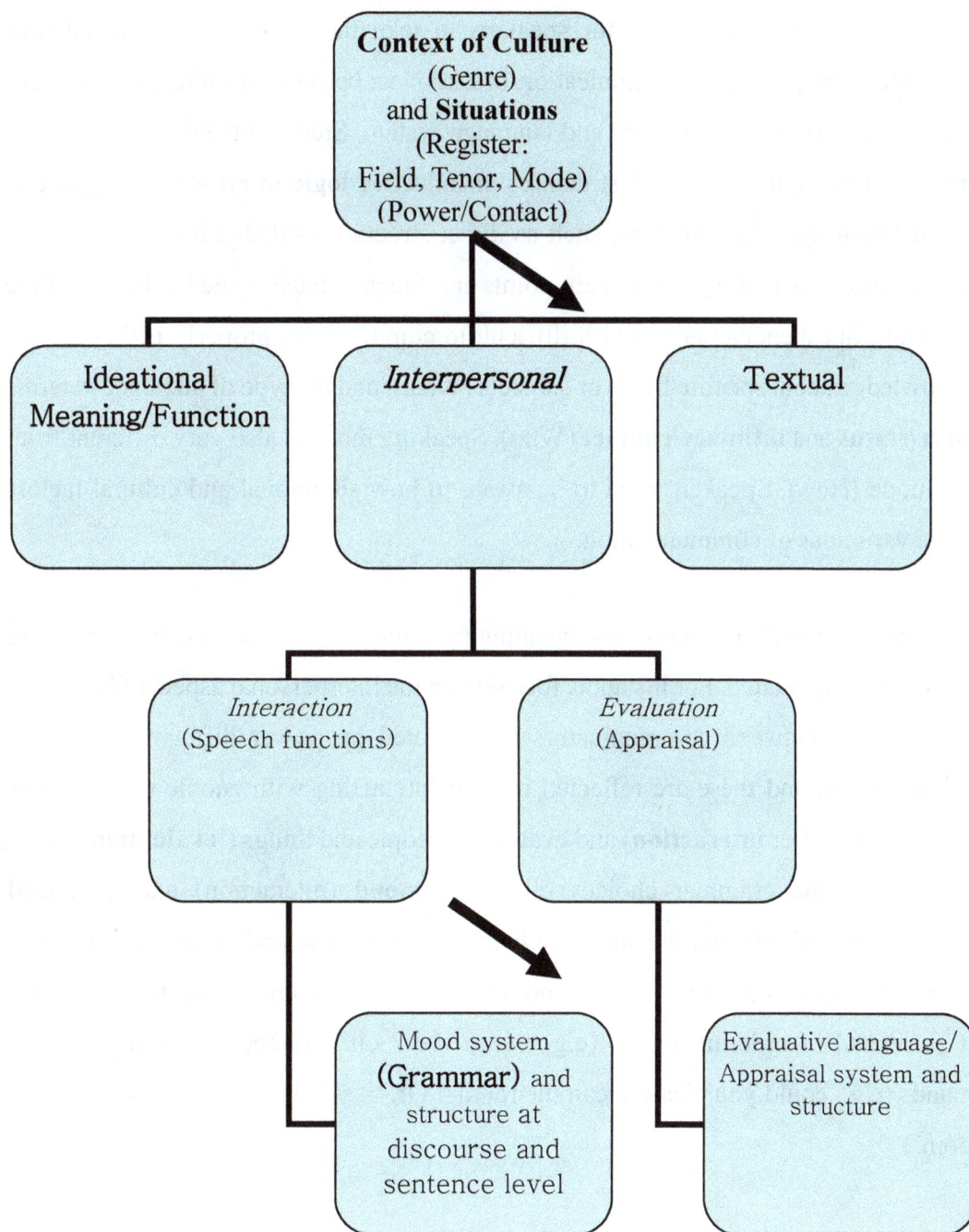

Figure 2: Systemic relationships between contexts, meanings and grammar focusing on an interpersonal aspect

Since this book is written in a speaking context, I will discuss the theory in this context mainly, focusing on the interpersonal function. In order to converse with people successfully, it is very important for speakers to take the context into account. For instance, speakers can have communication breakdowns because of cultural differences that are reflected in speech structure and language system. Students from Asian cultures, for instance, tend to use 'indirect' structures or inductive logic in presenting argument. This is different from the structure, such as direct structure or deductive logic, used in Western culture, where the general main points are directly stated at the beginning of the conversation. Speakers can also find it difficult to communicate properly if they do not have knowledge about specific fields or subjects (What), and the type of audience in terms of **power/status** and **intimacy/contact** (Who). Speaking mode is also very different from writing mode (How). Speakers need to be aware of how situational and cultural factors affect the variations of communication.

From the SFL point of view, contexts, meaning (semantics) and grammar (syntactic) are systematically interrelated. For instance, focusing on the interpersonal aspect of language, the relationships between communicators are affected by power differences and the degree of contact, and these are reflected in their interacting with people ('**interactive negotiation**'/hereafter **interaction**) and evaluating people and things ('**evaluation**'). This, in turn, affects the grammar choices related to **mood** (interaction) and **appraisal** (evaluation) respectively and the structure both at the sentence and discourse level. For instance, if a speaker has higher status and intimacy than a listener, s/he tends to use a direct command in ordering things (e.g. 'clean the room') rather than using indirect commands (e.g. 'could you please clean the room?' Or, 'it would be a good idea to clean the room').

In terms of the '**Linguistics**' element, while the SFL approach takes contexts into account a great deal, its primary focus is on linguistics (Woodward-Kron, 2005, p.25). Therefore, teaching grammar explicitly in an appropriate context plays a key role in its pedagogy. The approach is thus distinguished from situational/functional notions of teaching speech to some degree. While SFL takes into account language use being semiotic, functional, semantic and contextual, teaching grammar also plays a key role in its pedagogy.

Summary of the SFL approach

1. What approach is SFL primarily based on in regards to the use of language?

2. How is the SFL approach of functional grammar different from the traditional grammar approach and psycholinguistic based approaches such as the cognitive expressive approach and the process-based approach?

3. According to SFL, what are the two main contexts that have an impact on the creation of text? Explain.

4. What are the three meanings or functions that language allows us to convey?

5. What does 'text' mean from the SFL perspective and how can both structure and language system be interpreted from an interpersonal perspective?

6. How are context, meaning and grammar systemically linked to each other?

1.2. Interpersonal meaning within SFL

One of the main functions of (the English) language is to convey interpersonal meaning to people around us. That is, from an interpersonal perspective, the most important reason why learners are keen to learn English is to have successful communication with others. Communication can take place for the purpose of achieving two main goals (see Figure 1). One goal is to 'interact' with people when exchanging information and goods & services (**Interaction**).

When speakers would like to **exchange information,** they mostly use questions that contain six prompts of WH questions: what, when, why, how, where, and who (e.g. where are you from?) and then listeners respond to the speakers by using statements (e.g. I come from China). When speakers want to **exchange goods and services,** they make a request by using questions (e.g. Can I borrow the pen? [a Good]) or commands (e.g. please send the letter to me [a Service]). That is, interaction fulfils **four speech functions or roles** of English, namely statements, questions, commands and offers. Halliday (1994) claims that when language is used to exchange information, the clause takes on the form of a **proposition, which has informational value** in the exchange. When the clause is structured to enable the exchange of goods and services, it takes the form of **a proposal, which has interactional value**. Offers and commands are thus grouped together as **proposal**, and statements and questions as **proposition** (see Figure 3). The grammar to express the functions is known as '**Mood**'. Mood is expressed in a grammar that is declarative, interrogative, or imperative respectively (see Halliday & Matthiessen, 2004; Lee, 2010a). The concept of proposal is very important in explaining how to make requests/recommendations or provide advice in an appropriate manner. From an interactional perspective, all English sentences encode either proposals (he should come) and propositions (he will come).

Summary of Interpersonal Meaning

1. From an interpersonal perspective, what are the two main purposes of using language?

2. From an interactional perspective, what are the two main reasons for using language?

3. What are the four speech functions?

4. What are proposals and propositions?

5. What is mood? What are grammatical forms of speech functions?

Notes:

1.3. An overview of the Appraisal theory

The Appraisal theory divides evaluative linguistic resources into three main categories: **ATTITUDE**, **ENGAGEMENT** and **GRADUATION**. While **ATTITUDE** involves adopting subjective positions, **ENGAGEMENT** involves managing and negotiating intersubjective positioning. **GRADUATION** involves intensifying or downgrading a given value (see Figure 3). Let me explain these in more detail.

Another significant reason why people use English is to 'evaluate' things and people as well as to express their feelings and emotions (**Evaluation**). When speakers take up such positions, they express their subjective/individual opinions or views to listeners (e.g. Sydney is *beautiful*; He is a *conman*, I am *happy*, etc.). This function is called **ATTITUDE**. SFL divides the ATTITUDE function into 3 aspects. Firstly, it is reflected in **expressing our negative or positive emotions and feelings** (**AFFECT**); secondly, it is manifested in **judging behaviour** (**JUDGEMENT**); thirdly, it is reflected in **assessing things, entities processes** either positively or negatively (**APPRECIATION**). These three meanings of evaluations constitute the ATTITUDE system (see details, Martin 2000; Hood, 2006, 2010; Martin & White, 2005/2007; Martin & Rose, 2003/2007; Lee, 2008c). People reflect their attitude when choosing positive and negative evaluative expressions. When they use the attitudinal evaluations, they demonstrate their subjective views through positive or negative affirmations.

People also use English to adjust and negotiate their positions or views in order to engage in a dialogue with others. From an **ENGAGEMENT** perspective, we are thus concerned with whether all proposals or propositions are monoglossic (e.g. Sydney *is* a multicultural city) or heteroglossic (e.g. It *seems* that Sydney is a multicultural city; Martin *argues* that Sydney is a multicultural city). Under the monoglossic option, speakers use a bare assertion by rejecting further negotiations with listeners. However, heteroglossic options enable speakers to position themselves intersubjectively in an explicit manner (see Figure 3). If a speaker does not consider the listener in their talks, s/he does not need to use the resources. The resources therefore create 'humility' or 'persuasion' in their discourse.

This involves both showing speakers' willingness to negotiate with listeners whose views may differ and creating persuasion.

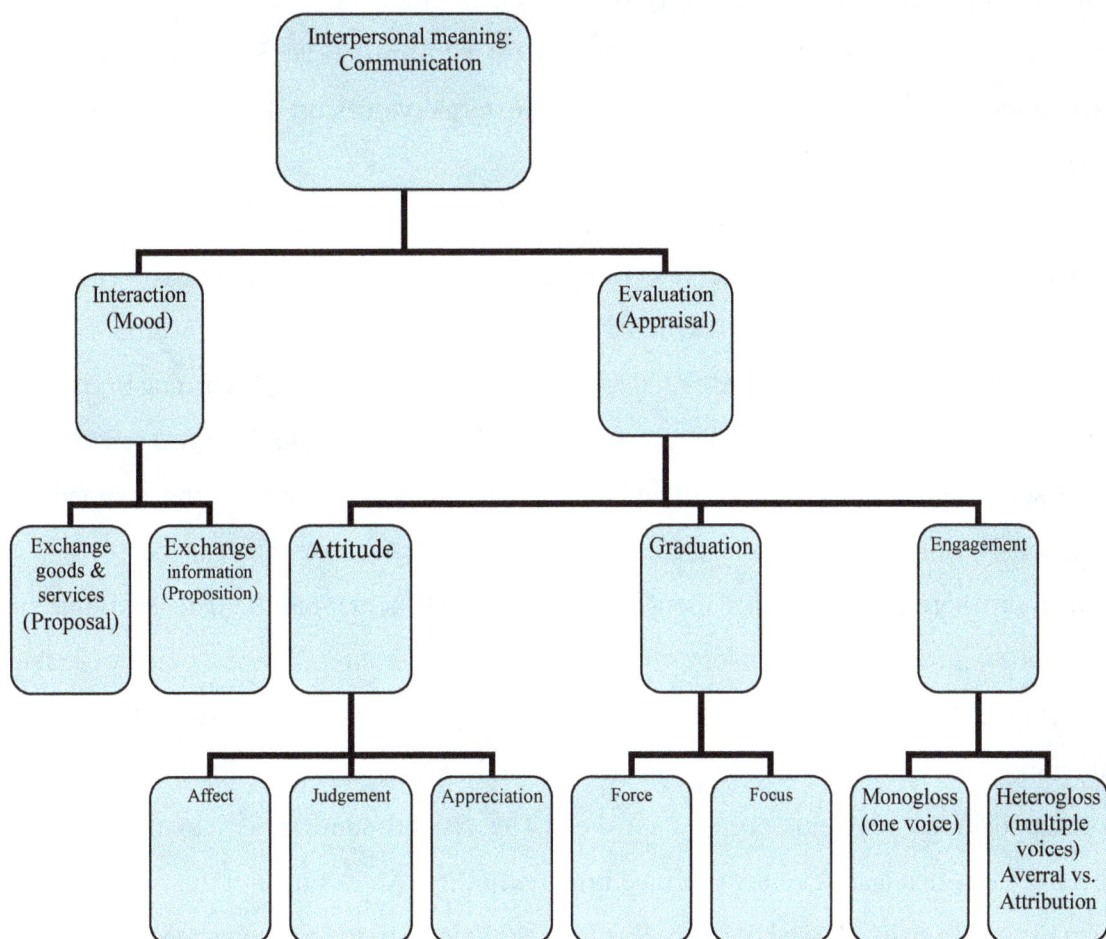

Figure 3: Two main reasons for using English from an interpersonal perspective

One way of making this adjustment is by speakers utilising other voices that come internally (**averral**). These include such resources as 'causes and effects' (e.g. because, as a result), 'concessions' (although, despite), 'countering' (e.g. however, on the other hand, 'time' (e.g. since, when), 'conditions' (unless, if), 'modality' (e.g. maybe, probably, it appears/seems that…), 'other metadiscoursal language' (e.g. I would say that…. The fact is that…), etc. For instance, when a speaker makes a positive or negative statement, a reader may react to this. So the speaker employs 'cause' resources (e.g. because, the reason being is that) to justify their position so that the listener may agree with them. Another example is that speakers use a 'concession' such as 'although' because they would like to acknowledge others' views prior to putting forward their opinions. Another way is to attribute the responsibility of their claims to some external voices by using citations or quotations to persuade listeners (**attribution**) (e.g. Kim claims that …; according to Kim, etc.). All these internal and external voices used to persuade listeners are called **ENGAGEMENT.**

ENGAGEMENT systems are derived from Bakhtin's notions of **heteroglossia** (multiple voices) and **dialogism or intertextuality** (see details, White, 1998, 2004; Martin & Rose, 2003/1007; Martin & White, 2005/2007; Lee, 2006, 2008a, 2010b). According to Bakhtin (1981, 1986), all texts, whether they are spoken or written, are dialogic in two senses. The first sense refers to the dialogue that occurs when a speaker answers and responds to previously uttered texts while anticipating responses. An example can be seen in a situation where a speaker talks about the September 11 incident to the listener. Based on previous knowledge, the dialogue between the speaker and listener will be further developed. However, if there were not prior dialogues between the two, the speaker's utterances to the listener about the incident would be very different due to the fact that presuppositions have not been established. The second sense refers to the dialogue between one text and other texts termed **intertextuality**. An example of this second sense can be seen in a situation where a speaker uses explicit quotes to convince readers. That is, when the speaker talks, they integrate other people's speech into their voices to convince the listeners.

Intertextuality forms one of the crucial grounds, especially for writing studies and writing practice. Texts do not appear in isolation, but in relation to other texts. We write in response to prior writing, and as writers we use the resources provided by prior writers. When we read, we use knowledge and experience from texts we have read before to make sense of the new text, and as readers we notice the texts the writer invokes directly and indirectly. Our reading and writing are in dialogue with each other as we write in direct and indirect response to what we have read before, and we read in relation to the ideas we have articulated in our own writing (Farmer, 1998; Hall et al., 2005; Bazerman, n.d.). From a dialogic/engagement perspective, the skillful balance/integration/merge/dialogue/incorporation between the interior (Averral) and exterior (Attribution) voices along the structure can contribute to successful communication (Lee, 2010b).

In addition, when speakers use **ATTITUDE** and **ENGAGEMENT**, they can intensify (force up) or detensify (force down) expressions termed **FORCE** (e.g. this is *the most* delicious meal; this is the *least* yummy food). Examples of **FORCE** include 'graders' (the best, extremely, significantly, etc.), 'measures' of time (immediately, instantly) and amount (largely, much, many). They can also modify the values by **FOCUS** (He is a *true* friend versus he is *a kind of* friend; in particular, when it comes to, etc.). **FOCUS** involves scaling up and down. Under **FOCUS**, values are graded on a scale between 'core' and 'marginal' membership. Examples of **FOCUS** include 'authenticity' (e.g. own, purely, deep solely, etc.) 'specificity' (e.g. particularly, precisely, specifically, etc.) and focusing items (e.g., when it comes to, with reference to, with regards to, etc.) and focusing down (kind of sort of, to some extent, etc.). These grading up and down of values is called **GRADUATION** (see details, Hood, 2006, 2010; Lee, 2010c). The Appraisal system entails all of these three systems: **ATTITUDE**, **ENGAGEMENT** and **GRADUATION** (see Figure 3).

In short, while we seek information and goods and services, we **simultaneously** evaluate them by expressing our attitude or taking a position. For example, the following sentence can be analysed according to the appraisal system.

Original sentence	According to a survey, Sydney is ranked as one of the most desirable cities to live in.
Appraisal analysis	*According to* a survey [Engagement; evidence], Sydney is ranked as one of *the most* [Graduation] *desirable* [Attitude: + Appreciation] cities to live in.

This analysis can be coded as follows:

ATTITUDE			ENGAGEMENT		GRADUATION	
Affect	Judgement	Appreciation	Monogloss	Heterogloss	Force	Focus
		+ desirable		According to	The most	

In the sentence, the speaker not only sends the information that Sydney is a nice place to live in (Interaction) but also makes a positive comment (desirable: Attitude) about Sydney. The speaker also scales up his/her attitude (the most: Graduation) and uses an external source of statistics to convince listeners through using engagement resources (according to: Engagement). While the speaker displays a positive attitude with great conviction toward the proposition, s/he opens up negotiation simultaneously by attributing its responsibility to other sources. Appraisal systems are realised in grammar by using adjectives, verbs, nouns, and adverbs.

The Appraisal system is thus concerned with linguistic descriptions of evaluative language both at **the semantic and grammar** levels. The system is very useful in teasing out being critical from a linguistic perspective. That is, critical voice or stance from a speaker or writer is generated from using the three systems effectively in an appropriate context. While the ATTITUDE system can help speakers or writers to raise their **subjective opinions** or views, the ENGAGEMENT system can enable them to be aware of listeners' or readers' reactions or refutations **intersubjectively**. The crux of successful communication thus lies in how to have the right balance between 'argument' and 'persuasion' as well as 'authority' and 'humility'.

Practice of Appraisal analyses

1. He was so mean because he cheated on me several times.

ATTITUDE			ENGAGEMENT		GRADUATION	
Affect	Judgement	Appreciation	Monogloss	Heterogloss (averral/attribution)	Force	Focus

2. Although learning English is challenging to some degree, it is extremely rewarding at the end of the day.

ATTITUDE			ENGAGEMENT		GRADUATION	
Affect	Judgement	Appreciation	Monogloss	Heterogloss	Force	Focus

3. I feel very upset about his absolutely stupid behaviour in the meeting.

ATTITUDE			ENGAGEMENT		GRADUATION	
Affect	Judgement	Appreciation	Monogloss	Heterogloss	Force	Focus

4. According to him, Turkey is the most beautiful country.

ATTITUDE			ENGAGEMENT		GRADUATION	
Affect	Judgement	Appreciation	Monogloss	Heterogloss	Force	Focus

5. It seems that he is a conman.

ATTITUDE			ENGAGEMENT		GRADUATION	
Affect	Judgement	Appreciation	Monogloss	Heterogloss	Force	Focus

Summary of the Appraisal system

1. What are three subsystems of the Appraisal system?

2. What are three subsystems of ATTITUDE?

3. What are the two broad subsystems of ENGAGEMENT? Give a sample sentence of each category.

4. What does 'intertextuality' mean?

5. What is the difference between ATTITUDE and ENGAGEMENT?

6. What are the two sub systems of GRADUATION? Give examples.

7. How can critical voice or stance be created from a linguistic perspective?

Section 2: A brief introduction to the main theory: ATTITUDE

ATTITUDE is one of the three main appraisal resources and it is considered to be the most important way that speakers can convey their evaluations. Consequently, in this book, I have chosen to concentrate solely on words that help us to express our subjective attitude. However, I have restructured those expressions to adjectival words that end with 'Y'. This is because such expressions are a commonplace feature of Australian English, especially everyday spoken interaction, yet cause ESL learners considerable difficulty.

On the basis of the three types of ATTITUDE, namely Affect, Judgement and Appreciation, we use English to express our positive and negative attitude explicitly and implicitly. I will now give some examples of words/phrases that express AFFECT, JUDGEMENT and APPRECIATION (see Figure 3 below).

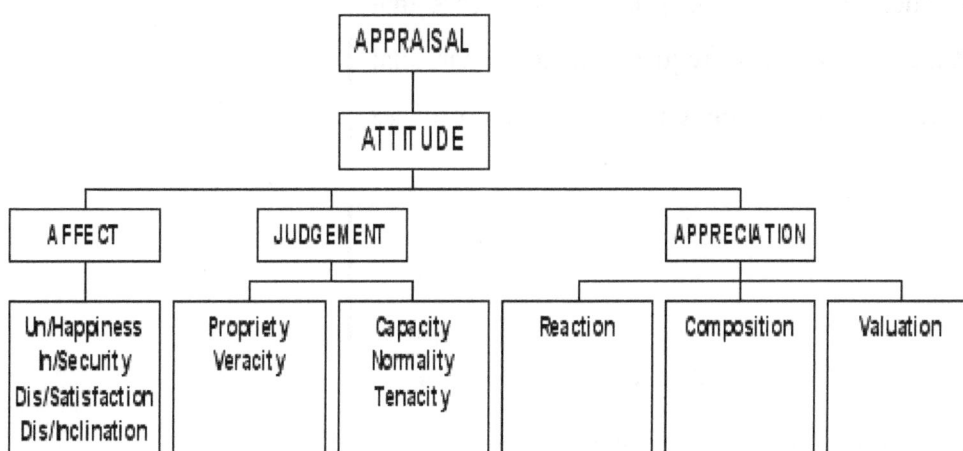

```
                          ┌───────────┐
                          │ APPRAISAL │
                          └─────┬─────┘
                          ┌─────┴─────┐
                          │ ATTITUDE  │
                          └─────┬─────┘
        ┌───────────────────────┼───────────────────────────────┐
   ┌─────────┐            ┌──────────┐                    ┌──────────────┐
   │ AFFECT  │            │ JUDGEMENT│                    │ APPRECIATION │
   └────┬────┘            └────┬─────┘                    └──────┬───────┘
        │              ┌───────┴───────┐           ┌─────────────┼─────────────┐
┌────────────────┐ ┌──────────┐ ┌──────────┐ ┌──────────┐ ┌─────────────┐ ┌──────────┐
│ Un/Happiness   │ │ Propriety│ │ Capacity │ │ Reaction │ │ Composition │ │ Valuation│
│ In/Security    │ │ Veracity │ │ Normality│ └──────────┘ └─────────────┘ └──────────┘
│ Dis/Satisfaction│ └──────────┘ │ Tenacity │
│ Dis/Inclination│              └──────────┘
└────────────────┘
```

Figure 3: ATTITUDE resources within the 'Appraisal' system

Before looking at how the ATTITUDE system can be implemented in casual expressions that end in 'Y', I would like to mark them in various ways. The following table explains some symbols used in the book to indicate several ways of differentiating Y-related expressions.

Key concepts and terms	**Bold**
Key Y expressions	***Bold & Italic***
Other Y expressions	*Italic*
Word collocations of Y expressions	*<u>Italic + Underlined</u>*
Other related expressions, idioms and words that are useful to be learned	• <u>Underlined with bullet points</u>
Important speech grammar + expressions, idioms and words. These focus on the grammatical errors that ESL students make most frequently or grammars that are useful for improving conversation as well as writing. The most important grammar used in Y expressions is marked with the * symbol. This symbol indicates that it is singled out for special attention and practice in separate boxes. In these boxes the most error-prone grammar is highlighted using **bold.**	<u>Underlined</u>
Nouns that are abbreviated into a 'Y' form are listed in Section 4, and the # symbol is used to mark these nouns in previous sections.	

2.1. AFFECT

Firstly, we use English in everyday life situations to express our **emotions and feelings either negatively or positively**. This is called AFFECT. AFFECT can be sub-classified into four dimensions.

2.1.1. Un/Happiness

I felt like *jumping over the moon* when I heard the news that I got promoted.

I *feel very excited about* attending my graduation ceremony.

I am very *upset about* what has happened to me lately.

2.1.2. Dis/satisfaction

I *am full*. I cannot eat anymore.

I was *extremely tired*. I was *completely flat out*. So I *slept like a log* yesterday as soon as I went to bed.

2.1.3. In/security

I feel *at home and comfortable* living in Sydney although the city is not my home town.

I feel *terrified* at the scene of a crime/an accident.

I felt completely *freaked out* when I saw the incident.

2.1.4. Dis/inclination

This has to do with a **'potential future event'**. This is different from the three previous AFFECTs, as they involve 'reaction' to an event in **the present or past**.

I am *willing* to learn English, while he is *very reluctant* to do so.

Although the students *are eager to* engage in the activity, _____

Even though the students *are keen on* studying, _____

He *is anxious to* complete his studies as soon as possible (desire for the future-Inclination).

He is *anxious about* the exam result (reaction to the past-Affect Insecurity).

2.2. JUDGEMENT

Secondly, we use evaluative language in order to **judge people's behaviour.**
JUDGEMENT can be made on the following five aspects of human behaviour.

2.2.1. Un/ethical (Propriety)
It is related to whether a person is **ethical or unethical.**

He is a *reliable* person, because he always keeps his word.

He is a *law-abiding* person, as he always observes/follows the rules.

It is not acceptable when you *cheat* in your exam.

2.2.2. Un/truthful (Veracity)
It has to do with how the person **is truthful or honest.**

As long as she acknowledges her mistakes, she is considered to be a very *honest* person.

He is a *conman*, because_____

He is an *unscrupulous* man, because_____

My supervisor is *sneaky* and *cunning*, because_____

2.2.3. In/capable (Capacity)
We are judging how the person is **capable.**

He is very *capable of playing the piano*, because_____

He is so *dumb*, because_____

2.2.4. Ab/normal (Normality)
It *is concerned with* how **the person is usual or special.**

The girl is lovely but she is so *weird* sometimes.

Since he has an *eccentric* personality, he_____

2.2.5. Un/determined (Tenacity)
We are judging how **the person is persistent, determined or dependable.**

While he is so *determined*, he is sometimes *indecisive*.

He is *a hard worker*, but sometimes he is *not conscientious*. He is *slack*.

2.3. APPRECIATION

Thirdly, English is used to **assess or appraise things, objects, entities, products and processes,** either positively or negatively. This is called **APPRECIATION.** APPRECIATION is also divided into three aspects:

2.3.1. Un/Appealing (Reaction)

It is concerned with whether or not **the thing grabs our attention or appeals to our emotion.**

This food was so *yummy* that I ate it all by myself. However, I do not like eating the bread, because it tastes *yucky*.

While the movie is *entertaining, it is a bit boring* at the beginning.

2.3.2. Un/balancing (Composition)

It <u>focuses on</u> whether or not the things or processes **have balance or not and are simple or complicated.**

Things are getting *complicated*, because_____

Students' writing is too *lengthy and messy*. So I cannot understand it.

The theory is *not systematically presented,* so it confuses me.

2.3.3. In/significant (Valuation)

It has to do with whether or not the thing **has social significance or worth**.

In order to get a job in South Korea, it is vitally *important* to <u>have a good command</u> of English.

It is crucially *essential* to speak English fluently to get a good job.

Too much use of detergent is *harmful* to the environment, because <u>it has a *detrimental* effect on waterways, plants and animals.</u>

Some key points need to be made in using ATTITUDE values. As already noted, all ATTITUDE items involve either positive or negative evaluations. It is thus very important to use evaluative language appropriately because speakers' choices make listeners react to the utterance positively or negatively too. Another key point is that it is sometimes not clear what the target of the evaluation is. It can be judging people's behavior (thus Judgement) or assessing things or processes (thus Appreciation). For instance, in the expression, "well done, good work, your work is so fabulous", here it can point to the person's ability or the work itself. There are also some overlaps among the three sub-categories of ATTITUDE. For instance, when someone is *cranky*, it can refer to the person's behavior (thus Judgement abnormality) or it can refer to the emotion (thus Affect unhappy). Another consideration is that evaluation can be explicit or implicit. For example, the sentence 'Your room is so *dirty*' is an explicit evaluation. Sometimes, evaluations can be made very subtly. Your room *is full of rubbish* (implicit or token). This means the room is not so tidy.

Most importantly, I follow the SFL approach that context is critical to conveying meaning. Consequently, the words I have chosen are words used in everyday conversation in Australia. In this context, some meaning may be surprising, but familiarity with the words will greatly advantage ESL/EFL speakers.

Summary of ATTITUDE

1. What are the three subsystems of ATTITUDE? Explain the functions of them.

2. What are the four subcategories of AFFECT? Give some positive and negative examples.

3. What are the three subcategories of JUDGEMENT? Give some positive and negative examples.

4. What are the three subcategories of APPRECIATION? Give some positive and negative examples.

Section 3: Practices of ATTITUDE in casual conversation

Unit 3.1 AFFECT
3.1.1. Un/Happiness

<u>Negative</u>

1)   Sulky

The girl is ***sulky*** very often. She does not speak when she is angry at her mum.

She is in a ***sulky*** mood.

The dog was ***sulky*** because it got yelled at by his owner.

Instead she just acted like a rather ***sulky*** teenager, whose boyfriend had deserted her.

She looked ***sulky*** all morning because she was angry about <u>the way her mother told her off</u>.

- Do not take his words personally, that is <u>the way</u> he speaks to everyone.
- I was very offended by <u>the way</u> he treated me.

The girl is *sooky* and cries all the time. Leave her alone. She is *having a sook.*

2)   Cranky

My husband is ***cranky*** this morning <u>for no reason</u>.

My husband has a <u>*bad temper*</u> and he *gets cranky* easily whenever I ask him to wash the dishes.

On my return I apologized for being so ***cranky*** and I guess the strain of the last couple of days was showing!

Jenn, who teaches her children at home, would become ***cranky***, tired and irritable during the day.

Depending on their mood, women often tend to *feel **cranky***.

- When babies need sleep, they begin to <u>*chuck a temper tantrum*</u>. [cf. Do not <u>*chuck rubbish away*</u> out of the house without considering what can be recycled].

3)   Grumpy

He is very *grumpy* today <u>for some reason</u>. He is in very *<u>low spirits</u>* today.

The guy is always *<u>grumbling</u>*. He needs to view things positively.

You look very *grumpy* today. What is wrong with you?

She is a bit nervous and can get a bit *grumpy* so needs to be in a home without young children or other cats.

He is a *grumpy* old man.

There are* several issues that the **grumpy** person needs to be deal with.

[Grammar 1: Relative pronouns (Embedded clauses)]

Examples:

<u>Defining</u>

There are many international students **who are** studying overseas.

There are many international students **studying** overseas.

There are many books (**that were) written** in English.

There were many books **written** in ancient Egypt.

Sample essays (**that were) written** by students are available in the library.

Sample essays **written** by students are available in the library.

<u>Non-defining</u>

Japan, which has suffered from continuous earthquakes, has been inundated with aid agencies.

Japan, suffering from continuous earthquakes, has been inundated with aid agencies.

The driver, who died instantly, was a close friend of mine.

4) Grouchy

I am sorry to be so *grouchy* today.

He has a bad temper and is very *grouchy* all the time.

Most people feel *grouchy* and uncertain about life after retirement.

Are you *grouchy* or irritable? Do you fall asleep driving? If the answer is yes, read on.

The *grouchy* teacher told the students to work from their books.

Weight loss doesn't have to be about starvation, fighting hunger pangs, resisting cravings, getting *grouchy,* lethargic, and suffering through headaches.

5) Huffy

My sister is a *control freak*. She does not take my ideas and feelings into account. If I don't do everything her way, she get very annoyed and *huffy*.

Now, don't *get huffy*. I was only *teasing*.

The comedy is about a *huffy* actress who loudly protests every perceived insult, no matter how slight.

6) Whingy/whiney

My husband is always *whinging/whingy*.

He complains when I make even the smallest of mistakes.

He is always *whining*.

Stop *whinging*. [cf. There is a tendency that '*whinge*' is used in UK and Australia, '*whine*' is US].

The little puppy has been *whining* from early in the morning. He must be sick.

He is always *whingy* and blames me if things go a little wrong.

- He tends to pass the blame to me when things do not go well. He is *buck passing*.

- He *passes the buck* when things do not turn out the way he wants.

  [cf. Buck has several meanings: a) A US, Australian or New Zealand dollar. E.g. Give me five bucks/dollars); b) I was tempted to *pass the buck* by making someone else responsible].

He is always *whining*/complaining about the weather.

Quit *whining* and finish your dinner.

"I want to leave now," she *whined.*

The workers were *whining* that the office was too cold.

The dog was *whining* because it wanted to go out.

7)   Gloomy

You look ***gloomy/melancholy***.

You *look depressed*. Come on <u>cheer up</u>, <u>chin up</u>.

What's wrong with you? Please <u>get it off your chest</u>.

Let's <u>have a chat and talk about it</u>.

<u>Don't hold it back</u>. Don't <u>bottle it up</u>.

You need to let it out. Otherwise, you <u>get stressed</u> and it makes you become sick <u>at the end of the day</u>.

8)   Moody

Teenagers are famous for being ***moody***.

He is so ***moody***. He makes me *feel rather down*.

I don't like men who are ***moody***. He *suffers from depression*.

Whenever he feels depressed, he has severe <u>mood swings.</u>

Sometimes he is up and then his mood goes down abruptly.

When <u>you are up</u>, you are <u>in a good mood</u> and you feel excited or joyful. When you <u>are down</u>, you are <u>in a bad mood</u>. You head hangs low, your shoulders sag and you might feel like crying.

9)   Mushy

That was a ***mushy*** love story. The movie was so romantic that I felt sentimental.

Cook until the fruit is soft but not ***mushy***. I do not like ***mushy*** food.

The peach was overripe and ***mushy***/*soft*.

The bottom of the pond is all ***mushy***/*wet* and feels awful when you stand up.

Take care not to overcook them as the flesh will become ***mushy***.

Mushy stuff; no *crunchy* stuff for me.

10) Teary

I become very *teary/tearful* when I am watching a soapie[#].

[cf Soapie is an abbreviation of soap operas. Australians use 'soapie' and Americans use 'soaps'/'soap'. It refers to TV dramas. Most Asians love to watch Korean soap operas (soapies)]. I love dramas/soapies. Korean soap operas/soapies/dramas are so fun. Once you watch them, you stay glued all day long. They are hooked on the dramas.

Kids love to watch the telly[#]/television. They are hooked on the Simpsons.

Watching the telly can become addictive.

- They stay glued once they begin to watch it. It becomes addictive.

- They are addicted to Korean dramas. They become Korean drama addicts.

- When they watch them, they cry as if they are in the same situation as the main characters.

11) Weepy

The teenagers got all *weepy* near the end of the film.

She started getting *weepy* when she talked about her mother.

I am *weepy* enough that I even cry at happy endings to movies and books.

He says he doesn't feel like going out with his friends and he is quite *weepy* a lot of the time.

Laura, with eyes still red and *weepy*, said, 'It isn't mine'.

Other days, she was depressed, exhausted, *weepy*, aggressive, irritable, dulled.

- When I hear that his parents passed away, I *take pity on* him.

- I am sorry to hear that. I feel sorry for him. [cf. When he heard the bad news, he passed out/fainted]. Commiseration.

12) Sappy/soppy

They easily become *sappy* and cry with little reason.

I feel *soppy/sappy*/sentimental whenever I listen to a love song.

I love to listen to *soppy* love songs.

Sometimes, I enjoy listening[*] to sad music. (See the box below for further grammar exercises in using an '-ing form after certain transitive verbs).

[Grammar 2: Transitive verbs that require an '-ing form]

Most transitive verbs are followed by both *-ing* form and 'to infinitive'.

Examples:

I begin to do this/ I begin doing this.

I continue to do this/ I continue doing this.

However, the following transitive verbs require only 'ing form:

We **delayed/postponed** launching the product because of technical problems.

I **look forward to** meeting you next week.

I don't **mind** staying late.

I really **enjoy** travelling abroad.

I have **finished** doing my assignments.

Students should **avoid** plagiarizing other work.

I **considered** quitting my job.

I will **stop** gambling.

I **quit** doing the work.

Positive

13)   Jolly

Santa Claus is a typical example of a *jolly* person.

My son is always a *jolly* guy. He looks cheerful.

He used to be a *happy* and *jolly* guy but because he is <u>going through puberty</u>, he is *grumpy* all the time.

Goodbye my love. I wish you had been here last night. We had an awfully *jolly* evening.

Jolly good chaps; let's go fight in the mountains of Afghanistan.

After the service, a very *jolly* ' tea ' party was held in the village hall, which was much enjoyed by all who attended.

14)   Smiley

She is always *smiley*. She always <u>*has a smile on her face*</u>.

Show your *smiley* face when I see you next time.

(cf. *Smileys* are also known as "emoticons". They are <u>glyphs</u> used to convey emotions in your writing. They are a great way to brighten up posts. 😃)

- You are bright and *chirpy* this morning [cf. The birds are chirping].

This area has been left deliberately blank for you to make notes or add other words.

Notes for Un/Happiness

3.1.2. Dis/satisfaction

<u>Negative</u>

15)   Weary

I become so **weary**, because he <u>keeps interrogating</u> me about the case. I *<u>feel drained</u>*.

She completely *<u>wears me out</u>*.

I need to rest my **weary** eyes.

The miners were **weary** after a long shift.

She was **weary** from years of housework.

16)   Achy

I feel all **achy.**

I have an **achy** back.

By evening I was beginning to feel restless and had really **achy** thighs so I had a bath with clary sage burning in the background.

When you catch a cold, you suffer from symptoms such as a runny nose, cough and temperature. You may feel **achy**.

I have **achy** feet by wearing shoes which are light, comfortable fitting and flexible.

17)   Stuffy

When I go into a small house, I feel very uncomfortable because the house is a **stuffy** space/place.

Open the car window. I feel sick. The car is very **stuffy.**

The swelling and fluid caused by blood and lymph vessel swelling <u>results in</u>[*] the symptoms of **stuffy** nose and *watery* eyes. (See the box below for further grammar exercises in cause and effect. This aspect of grammar is very important and yet students often find it difficult).

[Grammar 3: Causes and effects (ENGAGEMENT: Claim)]

- The government lowered the speed limit to 50 Km per hour. <u>As a result/as a consequence/consequently</u>, the number of traffic deaths decreased.

- The lowering of the speed limit to 50 Km per hour **resulted in** a decrease in the number of traffic deaths.

- The lowering of the speed limit to 50 Km per hour **led to** a decrease in the number of traffic deaths.

- The lowering of the speed limit to 50 Km per hour was the **cause of** the decrease in the number of traffic deaths.

- The lowering of the speed limit to 50 Km per hour was the **reason for** the decrease in the number of traffic deaths.

- The lowering of the speed limit to 50 Km per hour **had an effect on** the decrease in the number of traffic deaths.

- Recent climate change **has affected** people and nature in countless ways.

- Pollution in the air **has had a detrimental effect on** the environment.

- Recent climate change **has influenced/impacted (on)** people and nature in countless ways

- Recent climate **change has had an influence/impact on** people and nature in countless ways.

As the weather warms, spending *sunny* afternoons in a ***stuffy*** art museum hurts.

A ***Stuffy*** nose is caused by low oxygen in cells. Natural remedies are avoidance of allergies and breathing exercises.

Nasal congestion or '*stuffy* nose' occurs when nasal tissues and blood vessels become swollen with excess fluid, causing a ***stuffy*** feeling.

[cf. I have bought lots of stuff. I love this stuff/thing].

- You feel very frustrated when you can hardly express yourself in English (in other language 'stuffy' implies frustration).

18)   Dizzy

I have low blood pressure. That is why I get ***dizzy*** easily.

When you catch a cold, you get ***dizzy*** and get a headache.

Another major symptom is that you have a *runny* nose.

My nose is *runny*. I sneeze a lot. I am very *sneezy*.

- I need to take a sickie[#].

- How come you did not go to work today?

  I am having a sickie today. [cf. 'Sickie' is an abbreviation of 'sick leave'. Australians can be entitled to apply for a sickie once a month. Strictly speaking, the terms 'sickie' and 'sick leave' are different from each other. Sickie is used when you are not sick but pretend to be sick. Sick leave is used when you are genuinely sick. When taking sick leave, the person must bring a doctor's certificate].

- I am on study leave. I have deferred my study, because I have to go to the army. To serve at the army is obligatory, mandatory, and compulsory. Nobody can get away from it. It is unavoidable. So I put off my study for two years.

- You can't get away from doing this, you must do it.

19)   Dozy/drowsy

If you feel ***drowsy*** while driving from city to city, stop the car, get out and stretch your legs.

Too much alcohol can make you feel ***drowsy***.

I feel very ***drowsy*** when I take this pill.

The boy was so *drowsy* because his mathematics class was boring.

I felt *drowsy* after my long trip to the office.

We spent a *drowsy* afternoon by the pool.

I feel very tired. I slept late yesterday. So I <u>slept in</u> this morning.

I feel very *sleepy* today. So I nodded off when I attended the class.

20)   Dozy

I sometimes felt a little high and other times even *dozy*.

The big Thanksgiving dinner left us all feeling satisfied and *dozy.*

After I ate a big dinner, I felt *dozy*.

I hardly slept last night. When I attended the lecture, I dozed a lot, <u>*nodding off*</u> during the lecture.

21)   Dopey

Drugs make you feel very *dopey*.

Marijuana makes you feel *dopey/dopy*.

(cf. You are so *dopy*/stupid).

One of the Seven Dwarfs was called *dopey*, because he was a bit stupid not because he smoked *dope*.

Animals who feel secure and happy are *dopey* and relaxed.

The film is simply *dopey*, devoid of interest, and boring.

Obviously, making *dopey funny* films is his main source of cash.

<u>Positive</u>

22)   Happy

I am not *happy* with your job.

If you are not *happy* with this work, then I will do it again.

Your performance so far is not satisfactory.

23)   Comfy

You need to wear *comfy* shoes to go on a bush walk.

(cf. Comfy is an abbreviation of comfortable).

Just be yourself, dress in what you feel *comfy* in.

Look at the *comfy* armchair.

They may look *comfy*, but surely he doesn't expect to knock in many goals wearing these

This area has been left deliberately blank for you to make notes or add other words.

Notes for Un/Satisfaction

3.1.3. In/security

<u>**Negative**</u>

24)   **Clingy**

Your baby is so *whingy* and ***clingy*** today. What's wrong with him?

My girlfriend is always ***clingy***. She does not allow me to <u>focus on</u> my work.

I need my own breathing space.

When a person becomes annoying by always wanting to be around you, s/he just basically suffocates you.

I see why Robert doesn't like Kelly. She won't leave his fuckin' ass alone. What a ***clingy*** bitch!

25)   **Fidgety**

The student looks very ***fidgety*** today, as he <u>looks bored</u> with his work and easily becomes nervous when I ask a question.

When your child is ***fidgety*** and <u>restless,</u> try to distract him with some form of creative dramatics.

With mobile phone abuse at a high, he can't help but get a little ***fidgety***.

Children can be very ***fidgety*** and not able to stay in one place or complete an activity.

Sit still and stop *<u>fidgeting.</u>*

- The baby starts to *<u>fret/feel unhappy</u>* as soon as her mother goes out of the room.
- The baby looks uneasy, restless and *<u>fretful</u>* when her mum is not around.

26)   **Edgy**

She has been very ***edgy*** and nervous lately.

She is always *<u>on edge</u>* before an interview.

When people receive criticism, they tend to become very ***edgy*** and defensive.

Too much coffee makes me ***edgy***.

Why are you so ***edgy?***

Their relationship has always been ***edgy*** and tense.

27) Nervy

Since the new professor was appointed, my director has become very anxious and *nervy* about any email I send.

To make a public speech is so *nerve wrecking*. It is very burdensome. I get very *nervy*.

The passengers were restless and *nervy* after the long flight.

Too much coffee makes me *nervy*.

28) Scary

The movie was so *scary**. You scare me.

For him, hurricanes aren't *scary*, they are simply frustrating.

Not sure that will happen, but it's a *scary* possibility.

It's got to be a *scary* time for them because the movie contains lots of violent scenes.

- You are a *scaredy-cat*.
- I almost never win, so I am too much of a *scaredy-cat* to enter the contest.
- You are not courageous. You are a chicken.
- I *feel scared of** the fire.
- I am afraid of you because you are a dangerous person.
- She is afraid of falling off the mountain.
- I am scared of jumping out of an airplane since I could die.
- I am scared to* speak German with your family because I might say something wrong and not know it.
- Have you ever been scared of the dark?

[Grammar 4: As you have noticed, when people express their emotions and feelings (AFFECT), then the Past Participle adjective form is used. However, when evaluating things (APPRECIATION), then 'ing forms of adjectives are used.

I am scared of	The movie is scary or scaring
I am tired of driving I am tired with him	Driving is tiring He makes me feel tired
I am excited about the trip	The trip is exciting
I am surprised at the story	The story is surprising
I am disappointed at your work	Your work is disappointing
I feel burdened and stressed when I have to do assignments	Doing assignments is stressful/ burdensome
I **am interested in** taking the course Students **take an interest in** engaging in the activity	Doing the course is interesting The course interests me
I **am concerned about** him I **am concerned with**	The situation is concerning The situation **concerns** me The task concerns me

29) Panicky

Whenever I hear an alarming sound, I become ***panicky***.

When terrorists attack, the first thing you must do is *not panic*.

Stop being ***panicky***.

Please calm down. Keep your composure in any ***panicky*** situations.

Go on the attack and she risks being labelled ***panicky*** and desperate.

That isn't being fearful or ***panicky***; that is just good sense.

- *Panic attack* buttons are located on the top of the keypad.
- Sometimes moral panic can be created by certain individuals or groups.
- During Boxing Day, *panic buying* happened in David Jones.
- If you don't understand any of the terms above, *don't panic*.
- In *panic disorder*, the panic attacks may happen at any time.

30) Freaky

I was so scared of the dog. I hate dogs.

When I visited a friend of mine's house, the dog pounced on me. I was so *freaked out.* [cf. The terms 'scared of' and 'freak out' are almost the same but 'freak out' is an Americanism and is more associated with the drug culture of the 1970s].

I get so *freaked out* and *shaky*, when I see a car accident.

You *freak me out*. That is so ***freaky***. The movie is so ***freaky.***

The whole experience that I had in the country was really ***freaky***.

[Cf. Freak has a different meaning. He is a movie *freak*.

My daughter is a *clean freak*. He is a computer game *freak*.

My ex-husband is a control *freak*, so I ended up getting divorced.

I think Nicole is a control *freak* - she asked Keith to stop singing country music].

Koreans are footy *freaks.* They have footy fever.

31) Guilty

I feel very ***guilty*** about what I did to her.

I don't feel any sense of guilt, because I am innocent. I have been falsely accused of this.

This area has been left deliberately blank for you to make notes or add other words.

Notes for In/Security

3.1.4. Dis/inclination

32)   Needy

When women start feeling ***needy***, the feeling inside makes them feel helpless and powerless. Then anything a woman does or says just radiates that ***needy***, desperate vibe. That vibe again just pushes men away even more. It's like we spiral downward, get caught in quicksand and find ourselves in an endless loop. Women <u>cannot figure out</u> how to pull themselves out of that situation.

She was so ***needy*** but she was also *greedy* that this tended to drive men away.

You have to help those who are ***needy.***
The Salvation Army helps <u>the ***needy*** or people who are in need</u>.

This area has been left deliberately blank for you to make notes or add other words.

Notes for Dis/Inclination

Unit 3.2. JUDGEMENT
3.2.1. Un/ethical (Propriety)

Negative

1)   Bossy

Nobody likes her, because she is very **bossy**.

Stop being **bossy**, otherwise you cannot <u>find favour in your teacher's eyes</u>.

She is getting *bossier* as she gets older.

That might seem just a little **bossy** to us.

She is a **bossy** older sister.

She has finally found her spot within the group and has even started to become a bit **bossy**.

The horse is quite **bossy** and likes to get his own way.

When I was little, my brother *bossed* me around.

- If I can <u>find favour in your eyes</u>, I will do everything for you.
- The little brat is the teacher's pet.
- This is my favourite child.

2)   Bully

The **bully** <u>bosses you around</u> at school.

<u>School bullying</u> is a serious concern for all educators.

The guy is a terrible **bully**. He is quarrelsome and <u>overbearing</u> all the time.

I quit my job because I was being constantly **bullied** by my boss.

I recently have lodged *<u>a bullying complaint</u>* form against my supervisor.

When you are *bullied*, you need to <u>stick up for yourself</u> by saying firmly and confidently "Stop it".

When the hooligans *<u>mugged</u>* him, he fended them off by doing Taekwondo. He is so brave.

If you are raped, don't hide it. You need to <u>pluck up the courage</u> to tell the police what happened to you. You need to <u>stand up for</u> yourself.

- He is so mean and cruel. [cf. 'Mean' has other meanings. Once I say it, I mean it. I don't say something for nothing. Mean also is a mathematical average).

  When you want to receive unemployment benefits from the government, you have to make an appointment with a person in social security. What they do is they check your income and do a means test to see if you are entitled to receive money].

3) Bitchy

You are always so *bitchy* with me. I see how sweet and wonderful you are with friends, and with strangers, and yet you seem to save all *the bitchiness* for me. Why don't you just treat me the way you treat your friends?

That's not fair. I am not always *bitchy* to you.

You are *such a bitch.*

My wife is *bitching* at me all the time.

She is *a bitch.*

4) Nasty

My boss belittles me. He puts me down in front of people. He despises and belittles me.

He is so *nasty*. Don't be offended by his remarks. Get over it. That is the way he talks regardless of who he is talking to.

Regardless of/irrespective of who they are, what they are doing, where they come from, you've got to accept the person as they are.

Irrespective of colour, you should treat people equally.

My neighbour has a *nasty* dog that keeps barking at me.

I hate this smell of rubbish. It is so *nasty.*

He is a *nasty* teacher.

She is downright *nasty* to those who disagree with her views.

Before we get a bit too *nasty* we should probably talk about what happened first.

A particularly *nasty* strain of the virus can make normally healthy people very ill.

All I needed was something to relieve the pain from some rather *nasty* mosquito bites which I acquired.

The child has *nasty* habits like biting his nails or picking his nose.

If you see the world as a ***nasty*** place with evil around every corner, guess what?

- She always <u>speaks ill of</u> others. She is always <u>backbiting</u> and gossiping.
- She has a big mouth. She is a <u>busy body</u>. She is an extremely ***nasty*** lady.
- My maths teacher is <u>picking on</u> me for some reason. He <u>keeps teasing me</u> in front of all my friends.
- I <u>get so annoyed</u> at his ***nasty*** attitude.
- He is a bit of <u>a teaser</u> today.
- <u>Stop teasing</u> me otherwise I am not going to <u>put up with</u> it anymore.
- I <u>cannot stand it</u> anymore.

5)   Snobby

In general, pommies are very ***snobby/snobbish.***

Pommies refer to people from England. They are <u>so proud of</u> themselves.

No, I cannot agree with you there. <u>To some degree/extent</u>, everybody can be <u>arrogant</u> in different ways.

He tends to have a ***snobbish*** attitude. He is *snooty*. He <u>looks down on</u> people.

Snobby critics ironically make a very good living reviewing Hollywood movies!

Snobby people, they are so wrong!

The spinster is too ***snobby and picky.*** That is why she <u>has not been able</u>* to find <u>Mr Right</u> up to now.

[Grammar 5: Tense for double modals]

I can do this.

I was able to do this.

I have been able to do this.

I will be able to do this.

I must do this.

I had to do this.

I will have to do this.

Double modals:

I should be able to do this.

I might be able to do this.

I will be able to do this.

Modal in a passive form:

This can be done by me.

This must be done by me.

This should be done by me.

This **needs to be done** by me.

68

6) Haughty

From what I have seen, they are so ***haughty and snooty.***

He is boasting all the time.

- He is <u>bragging about</u> nothing.
- I am not bragging, but I can be very resourceful.
- <u>Stop bragging.</u>

7) Showy

Everybody stays away from him, because he is <u>showing off</u> all the time.

He is too smug and boasting.

He wears ***showy*** jewellery and clothes. He says like look at me, look at me!

He has a ***showy*** and expensive car.

8) Cocky

I hit the target on my first three attempts. Then I got a bit ***cocky*** [cf. A cock is a male chicken. They walk around with great pride, as do people who are acting or feeling ***cocky***]

Americans look very *friendly/neighbourly* but in fact they are very *cocky*.

They are <u>*arrogant*</u> in fact.

My favorite comedian is Yu JaeSuk because he looks very *friendly and neighbourly*. I feel comfortable with him.

That bloke has become very ***cocky*** and <u>arrogant</u> after his promotion.

9) Brassy

The criminal is very ***brash/brassy***.

He is <u>*brazen-faced and impudent*</u>.

Even though he <u>committed a serious crime</u>, he did not show any remorse to the victim. He acts as if he did not do that.

She is a bit <u>brash and audacious</u>.

It sounds <u>presumptuous/rude</u>, but can I <u>ask you a big favour?</u>

It might <u>be a big ask</u> but I would <u>appreciate it</u> if you could send it to me.

10)   Naughty

You are *naughty* if you muck around in your class without studying.

Stop mucking around here.

Stop mucking around. Get on with your work.

[cf. You have mucked up my life. You have screwed up my life. My life is completely screwed up because of you. This photo is mucked up].

He is a *naughty* (a negative term) boy.

This is my present for you. It's small but it is from my heart.

You are a *naughty* (a positive term) girl, you shouldn't do that.

I was told off by my mother for my *naughty* behavior.

- I was told off by my teacher because I misbehaved during class. She scolded me harshly.
- I was grounded by my parents when I got home.
- I will give you big trouble/you will be in big trouble if you don't listen to me.
- You will be grounded if you do not behave yourself.
- I was scolded by my teacher because I wagged classes too often.
- He was telling me off in front of my classmates.
- I play truant these days because I hang out with bad friends.

11)   Sleazy

She acts like a prostitute.

She could be hot and sexy, but she wears very *sleazy* clothes.

The man is devious.

He approaches you and tries to touch you. He is so *sleazy.*

He is out to get you. He is hanging around you all the time. Be careful.

12)   Skanky

She is very hot but *skanky.*

She wears *skanky* clothes.

13)   Flirty

She is a bit *flirty/flirtatious* whenever she sees men.

When women find sexually attractive men, they begin to flirt.

14)   Seedy

A *seedy* pub is smelly and unattractive. You feel uncomfortable there.

We eventually found the place which turned out to be a rather *seedy* looking underground car park.

They blame a recent drop in theatre attendances on the impression that the West End has become *seedy* in recent years.

15)   Kinky

He is a <u>pervert</u>. He must be *kinky*.

He is a *kinky* character.

He has a *kinky* taste in sex.

What *kinky* things have you done for your spouse/lover?

16)   Horny

Teenagers get *horny* when they see porno movies.

17)   Greedy

You ate the whole pizza. I don't believe it! You greedy pig! You are a *greedy* pig.

These are some real-world examples of *greedy* companies and individuals that put their own desire for wealth and possessions ahead of the needs of others.

These are all examples of *greedy* behavior. Any decision to take from others or to enrich yourself <u>at the expense of others</u> is an example of *greed* and is something that should be avoided at all costs.

18)   Stingy

He is so *stingy* and he never spends any money on us. He is <u>a miser</u>.

The company was too *stingy* to raise salaries.

Until his redemption, Ebenezer Scrooge is the classical example of a very *stingy*, heartless miser.

19) Pushy

Don't be too *pushy* with your children <u>when it comes to</u> studying.

<u>It doesn't work.</u>

This washing machine does not seem to function properly. This computer is out of order. It does not work.

In general, Asian countries value education a great deal but sometimes parents are too *pushy*. This <u>puts enormous stress on</u> children. That is no good. <u>What's the point of</u> pushing children like this?

You are too <u>harsh.</u>

Don't be too <u>hard on yourself</u>.

Don't be so *pushy*. Leave me alone. It is hard for me to hear you say that I am *pushy*. You are probably <u>feeling really pissed off at</u> me.

20) Nosey

Parents are too *nosey* as a result.

They <u>are too concerned with</u> *petty* matters.

- They <u>put/poke their noses into</u> all of their children's matters. They pry into their children's affairs and peep into their rooms.
- Children hate being told to do this and to do that by parents. This causes a reaction from children. Children often become rebellious.
- Keep your nose out of it.
- Don't <u>interfere with</u> them.

21) Granny

Mum, please don't be a *granny*. I know what I am doing.

[cf. Granny is an abbreviation of grandmother. In contrast, <u>nanny</u> is a person who takes care of a baby. I have hired a <u>nanny</u> to nurse my baby].

- I am sick and tired of her *<u>nagging like a granny</u>*.
- She *<u>keeps nagging</u>* me for no reason.
- <u>Stop nagging</u> me.
- I *<u>feel disgruntled</u>* when my boss asks me to do administrative work.

- I *get really annoyed* by my mother-in-law's nagging.

- She *is really a pain in the neck*.

- She is such a pest. My child *keeps pestering* me to buy the clothes.

- <u>Sorry for pestering</u> you but may I ask you a favour?

- Sorry for <u>bothering you</u>, but can you spare me a minute.

- <u>What bugs/bothers me is that</u> he did not reply to my messages.

- I <u>don't bother much</u> about that.

- Flies really annoy us when we have a Barbie# in the park in Australia. [cf.'Barbie' is an abbreviation of 'Barbecue' (BBQ). Let's have a barbie on the weekend].

- It *really irks* us and we feel irritable.

- They are *disgusting*. Snakes are really *disgusting*.

22) Snappy

Stop being ***snappy***. That's good for nothing.

Positive

23) Thrifty

He is ***thrifty*** and *frugal*.

My mum never wastes leftover food. She thinks that <u>chucking food away</u> is so wasteful.

<u>What a waste</u> if you <u>chuck food away!</u>. <u>Chuck away</u> this rubbish.

She is economical. She has to *scrimp on* toilet paper and shampoo to save money.

We *scrimped* and saved to buy our first home.

24) Worthy

I don't feel ***worthy*** enough to receive this award.

I am not ***worthy*** enough to pray to God.

It is not *worth investing* money in this. It is *not worthwhile to* invest money in this.

It is <u>no use doing</u> this. What's <u>the point of</u> doing this? I cannot see <u>any point in</u> studying hard.

25) Friendly

He is so **friendly**. He is warm-hearted, affectionate, and compassionate.

He has a big heart so you can lean on his big shoulders. He takes in everything I say. He is a very affectionate person.

The child is very *smiley*. Whenever I see him, he always smiles and gives me a big hug.

We received a *hearty*/big welcome from him when we visited his house.

He is so generous and hospitable. Thank you for your hospitality.

I feel like having a *hearty* meal at this time.

26) Lovely

My daughter is so **lovely**.

What **lovely** weather! It is *sunny* today. Beautiful.

This story is so touching and I was touched so much by his **lovely** present.

The couple are *lovey-dovey*.

- Some couples get along very well like a house on fire.
- But other couples fight like cats and dogs.

27) Homely

My daddy is very much a home body. He always comes home after work.

His landlady is a kind and **homely** woman.

The restaurant has a **homely** atmosphere. So I feel at home whenever I go to the restaurant.

28) Motherly

She is so **motherly**. Whenever I want to eat food, she serves me all the time.

The Asian lady in the restaurant is a kind and **motherly** woman, because she helps me to eat fish that has lots of bones.

This area has been left deliberately blank for you to make notes or add other words.

Notes for In/propriety

3.2.2. Un/truthful (Veracity)

29) Dodgy

The car mechanic is very *dodgy*.

He <u>ripped me off</u>. He overcharged me for repairing my car.

He is <u>untrustworthy</u>. He is <u>unreliable and unscrupulous</u>.

He is a bit of a *dodgy* doctor. He is <u>a quack doctor.</u>

The chair is a bit *dodgy*. Don't sit there.

30) Shoddy

He is a *shoddy* tradesman. He did a *shoddy* job. He cheats people because he charges money that he does not deserve.

- People are always <u>ripped off</u> by him**.**
- I realized that I <u>got ripped off</u> when I compared the money I paid for the bag with the money my friend paid.
- He is a <u>crook. He is dishonest</u> [cf. This knife is crooked /bent].
- The police chase crooks.
- I feel <u>crook</u> today, can I <u>have an *early* mark</u> today.
- All right I will give you a break. You can <u>have an *early* mark</u> today. But <u>one string/condition is attached</u>; you must do your homework. That's <u>fair enough</u>.
- He is <u>so crook</u> and he has to spend the night in hospital.

31) Tricky

He is a <u>conman,</u> but you would not know it. He is so deceptive.

He is very *tricky* and he looks like <u>a conman</u>.

I am going to use *a trick* to catch a thief.

He <u>conned</u> you by using *a trick*.

You <u>got conned</u> by the mechanic, because you were overcharged.

The essay questions can be very **tricky**. I do not know how to answer the questions.

I am in a <u>catch twenty two situation</u> at the moment, because I have no idea what to do.

When are you going to marry?

That's a very *tricky* question.

That is the <u>64 thousand dollar</u> question at the moment.

32)   Flimsy

He is telling a lie. He is so transparent. He always makes a *flimsy* excuse when he is <u>in</u> <u>trouble.</u> That's a very bad attitude. He needs to <u>fix it up</u>.

Could you <u>fix up</u> this tap, it has been leaking since last week.

You cannot build a boat only from tree bark. It would be too *flimsy*.

33)   Iffy

The meat smells a bit *iffy* to me. It must have gone off.

The student cannot attend the class, because his mother was sick.

It sounds a bit *iffy* to me. It is suspicious. He must be telling a lie.

I am doubtful/skeptical about his excuse.

Your man stops being *iffy* with you and tells you he loves you; then he does things that show otherwise.

34)   Fishy

He is a questionable character. He is so suspicious. Something *fishy* is happening with him.

 He must be a spy.

There must be something *fishy* going on/around here

<u>Own up</u>/confess.

Who did a fart/did someone pass wind? <u>Own up</u>.

35)   Quirky

He has some unusual quirks in his personality. He is a bit *quirky.*

He has a *quirky* sense of humour.

Did you see the program? It was a *quirky* TV show.

36) Grubby

Go and wash your *grubby* hands.

Some floor cushions look a bit *grubby* because children sit on them.

I went back to sleep, feeling slightly *grubby.*

We'll look very *grubby* indeed, won't we, *in comparison to* him?

37) Scabby

He is always begging for food here and there at lunchtime. He is *such a scab*.

In these days, many men <u>sponge off</u> women like parasites. They are *scabs/scabby.*

38) Sneaky

The tradesman deceives us secretly.

He is so *sneaky*. You can **sneakily** get out of here.

High school students *sneakily* watch m/X-rated videos.

The *sneaky* boy slipped outside to have a smoke without getting caught by his parents.

Once you get <u>caught red-handed</u> you will be in big trouble.

City people tend to be *sneaky.*

They are <u>city slickers,</u> while we are <u>country bumpkins.</u>

39) Speedy

Rats are so *speedy* and *sneaky* you <u>can hardly</u> catch them.

Don't *speed!* Don't drive over the speed limit, you can <u>get fined.</u> When I stopped in a non-stopping area, police approached me and <u>booked</u> me. I <u>got fined</u> $100. [cf. the weather is perfectly fine].

I was booked by the police. (cf. Can I <u>book</u> a room in your hotel?)

40) Crafty

He is very *crafty* and cunning/deceitful. He is so calculating.

I love doing *crafts*. He is a *crafty* man.

I hate my ex-wife so much because she was <u>sly</u> like a fox. Ex-husband, Ex-boyfriend, Ex-member. In Aesop's fables, 'the fox' is *crafty.*

This area has been left deliberately blank for you to make notes or add other words.

Notes for Veracity

3.2.3. In/capable (Capacity)

Negative

41) Geeky

School friends are <u>making fun of</u> you by saying you are *geeky.*

S/he is a <u>square </u>so s/he looks *geeky.*

Most scholars tend to be <u>pedantic</u>. They tend to <u>knit-pick about tiny details</u>.

Most of them are *geeky* .They do not have <u>well-rounded personalities</u>.

They have <u>their heads in the air</u>. They are not <u>down to earth.</u>

He is <u>a down to earth kind</u> of person.

I am still <u>up in the air.</u> I am still confused.

42) Nerdy

He only focuses on his study. He is *a nerd.*

My husband is *a kind of nerd*. He is a boring person. He is only interested in computers.

He also wears *nerdy* clothes that do not look fashionable.

If you are too serious about your study in Australia, you *get teased* by your classmates <u>rather than</u> get praised. S/he is a <u>machine</u>.

It sounds <u>odd/weird/strange</u>, but it is a fact of life.

It is so <u>weird</u>. It is really <u>warped</u>.

43) Airy-fairy

The politicians give *airy-fairy* descriptions in their political promises.

Blonde girls tend to have *airy-fairy* ideas.

They are <u>superficial, light and flippant</u>.

44) Wishy-washy

Most students have *wishy-washy* thinking that they will pass their subjects without putting in due efforts. These students <u>are likely to</u> fail in their studies.

Did he agree or not? It is hard to say. He gave a very *wish-washy* answer.

I loved this series but can't help thinking that this **wishy-washy** final episode lets the side down a bit.

The date techniques will help women handle their **wishy-washy** noncommittal man.

I recently realised that I like black music, but up until then I'd been a bit **wishy-washy.**

Knowing what you want is hot; if you're not **wishy-washy** a woman knows she's desired.

He *is inclined to* do the work. He has an inclination to_____

He *intends to* *study overseas. He *has the intention to* study overseas.

He *tends to* come late. He *has a tendency to* come late.

He *is likely to* come late.

Japan <u>is likely to</u> have an earthquake.

[Grammar 6: To infinitive or 'ing form]

Verbs that express desire or inclination only require the use of the 'to infinitive' and not an 'ing form. Examples are, 'tend to', 'is willing to', 'intend to' 'wish to', 'want to', 'hope to'. Other verbs of probability such as 'is likely to', 'appear to', 'pretend to', 'seem to' also require the use of the 'to infinitive' only.

The following examples of 'capacity' also are followed by the 'to infinitive' only.

I **manage to** complete my assignment.

I **attempt to** go overseas by myself.

I **cannot afford to** buy the house now.

I **decide to** attend the workshops.

He **offers to** give money to me but I **refuse to** accept it because it is considered to be bribery in my country.

I **neglect to** do the work, so I **deserve to** receive only a small salary.

However, the following inclination expressions require using 'ing forms or nouns rather than the 'to infinitive': be subject to/be prone to:

The area is subject to flooding.

The timetable is subject to change.

The country is prone to having earthquakes.

Japan is an earthquake prone country.

ESL learners are prone to making these grammatical errors.

I am a very *wishy-washy* type of person.

Don't be *wishy-washy* and make a careful plan <u>in advance</u>. You need <u>to preplan</u> it.

Don't make <u>an ad hoc</u> decision. You will face the consequences. You will <u>face the music</u>.

Think ahead/hard before you make any serious decisions.

45) Willy-nilly

Do not put the books *willy-nilly* on the bookshelf. Put them in alphabetical order. (cf. originally willy-nilly meant hesitantly, but now it means in a disorganized manner without direction or planning).

When the student went to his first week in university, he started joining clubs *willy-nilly*.

I can't find my keys or my wallet because I just leave things scattered about *willy-nilly*.

Politicians need to restrain themselves. They keep spending money on projects *willy-nilly.*

46) Clumsy

Most students are *clumsy* in using references when they first start their studies at university.

The job was done *clumsily* by you. I am very bad at doing this job.

My husband is very *clumsy* when <u>doing the dishes</u>.

A *clumsy* person always drops and spills things.

47) Hasty

You tend to always be *hasty.*

Don't <u>make haste.</u> Don't rush. Don't *hurry*.

He is always *in a hurry.* He is never relaxed. He needs to <u>take a rest</u>. I am *in a hurry*. I've got to go. I have to <u>hit the road</u>. Please take your time. Slow down.

I <u>used to</u>* work really hard, but now I have had to <u>slow down due to problems with my health.</u>

Do not make a *hasty* decision.

[Grammar 7: Use, used to (To infinitive), get use to ('ing form)]

I **used to live** in Seoul. Seoul is <u>one of the biggest cities</u> in the world. The <u>hustle and bustle</u> of the city is quite <u>overwhelming</u> at first. However, once you <u>get used to it, you will love it</u>. When I first visited a big market in Korea, I was so impressed. I love the <u>hustle and bustle</u> of the market.
But I did not like Korean food at first because too much hot chilly **is used** in the food, but once I **got used to** <u>eating</u> it, I loved it.

In the following examples, **to** is a preposition, so it is followed by the **-ing** form. Therefore, don't use a verb in the infinitive after the following expressions:

I **look forward to** <u>seeing</u> you soon.

I **devote myself to** <u>doing</u> this.

I **make strong commitments to** <u>attending</u> the workshops.

I have many **objections to** <u>transferring</u> his course at the moment.

Technology has **contributed to** <u>improving</u> our lives.

A positive aspect of education is that it **contributes to** <u>confirming</u> one's identity.

Positive

48)   Brainy

He is very smart and ***brainy.***

He is <u>dumb and thick</u>.

I like ***scholarly*** people.

49)   Savvy

Generation Y has been characterised as media and internet **savvy,** as they have practical knowledge of how to handle computers very well.

He is a computer **savvy.**

50)   Handy

He is a ***handyman***. He can fix everything. He is useful as he is a <u>go-getter.</u>

One thing that I like about Korea is that everything is so ***handy***.

Shops are open late at night so you can get access to shops conveniently.

In Australia, shops close early. Sometimes, it is <u>a real hassle</u> to drive to buy food.

- <u>What a hassle!</u> It is a real <u>nuisance!</u>
- What a <u>nuisance!</u>

I always carry a pen in my handbag. It often comes in ***handy***.

I received a bath towel as a present. That will be ***handy***.

51)   Sassy

She is so **sassy.** She looks slightly sexual.

New Yorkers are **sassy** and confident.

52)   Witty

He is very **witty** and humorous. He loves to joke.

You are joking/kidding.

Witty is *funny* in a clever way.

This area has been left deliberately blank for you to make notes or add other words.

Notes for In/Capacity

3.2.4. Ab/normal (Normality)

__Negative__

53)   Fussy

My mother-in-law is very *fussy*.

The school excursion is still three weeks away but my son has already been *making a big fuss* about it.

My husband also *makes a big fuss* about small things.

They always <u>make a big deal out of nothing.</u>

Don't *make a big fuss* out of nothing. Why are you <u>making a big deal</u> about it? That's no big deal. He is making <u>a storm in a teacup.</u>

My arm hurts. It got bruised. Please put cream on my arm.

Ouch. Don't be *fussy*/don't overreact.

I am not *very fussy* about correcting your grammar <u>at this stage.</u>

54)   Finicky

My girlfriend is so *fussy and finicky* all the time so we broke up.

I <u>was dumped</u> by my boyfriend.

We <u>broke up</u> a couple of weeks ago but we <u>made up</u> soon after.

It is very *finicky* to fix up this resume.

- If you want to get a good job, the first thing you need to do is to polish your CV (Curriculum Vitae).

55)   Picky

My son is too *picky/choosy* with his food.

My *hubby* is so <u>fastidious.</u> [cf. hubby is an abbreviation of husband].

<u>When it comes down to</u> buying clothes, I am very *choosy*/**picky.**

He is usually <u>laidback</u> but <u>when it comes down to</u> money, he is very *picky* and critical.

Australians are usually <u>laidback.</u>

<u>When it comes down to</u>*<u>learning English,</u> there are no short cuts.

[Grammar 8: Focusing on items or things (GRADUATION: FOCUS)]

Moneywise, he is so critical.

As far as money **is concerned**, he is so critical.

With regard to money,

With respect to money,

With reference to money,

Regarding money,

Concerning money,

In relation to money,

Relating to money,

Focusing on money,

In terms of money,

When it comes to money,

56) Choosy/Choosey

How is your job hunting going? You cannot be too *choosey*.

I have to be very *choosy* at this time when I am job hunting/trying to find a job.

57) Loopy

He will *go loopy* when he hears the news.

My boss will be *loopy* and furious when I refuse to do the work he has asked me to do.

I tried to reassure him that I'd be okay, but I was already acting *loopy* from the poison.

I use the term '*loopy*' to mean strange, not acting normally, *crazy*, as 'in the guy was a bit *loopy*'.

Let's examine how *loopy* logic leads to *loopy* behavior when we allow our primitive and emotional brain to deal with worry without the help of our rational brain.

58) Loony/Looney

They are *loony/crazy* as their behaviour is strange.

In the movie Hulk, the man *goes loony* when the moon changes.

He must be *a loony* because he grins at everyone.

Somehow, people who fight for rights and justice always get labelled with silly names such as '*loony*' and `eccentric'.

Every family includes someone who's a little *loony.*

The bull *went loony* when he saw the red flag.

- I just hit the roof because I was so upset about what he said.

59) Crazy

I *go crazy* when my wife keeps demanding this and that.

- She is very demanding. Doing assignments in Australian universities is very demanding and challenging.
- The crowd went *crazy* when the Beatles stepped out on stage.
- She is *crazy* for him.
- He drives me nuts.
- I am just out of my mind.

- I am <u>beside myself</u> with anger.
- I <u>go mad/nuts/bananas</u>.

60) Wacky

Wacky means *funny* or amusing in a slightly *crazy* way.

Some of his friends are pretty wild and **wacky** characters.

That motive was really **wacky** and strange.

The question is, <u>*why on earth*</u> would rational, sane and sensible people be so influenced by weird and **wacky** stories?

If you think this sounds a bit **wacky**, I'd have to agree.

He has <u>*gorgeous*</u> hands, with some really **wacky** silver rings.

I searched the web in an attempt to choose a school that didn't seem too **wacky**.

61) Touchy

I can understand your feelings but you are so **touchy**/*sensitive* and you are the type of person who <u>gets easily offended/hurt</u> by little things.

<u>The way he talks</u> is very <u>provocative</u>.

I don't like <u>the way he thinks.</u>

He <u>stirs me up</u> and I get <u>so upset</u>.

When I feel like <u>enough is enough</u>, I <u>hit the roof</u>. I <u>lose my temper</u>.

I <u>am about to</u> hit the roof/I am <u>about to</u> explode.

He <u>is about to</u> go. He is <u>on his way</u>. He has just gone.

I was <u>almost about to smack/</u> hit her but I stopped.

62) Shy/coy

The Greek couple are very <u>outgoing, sociable and gregarious</u> (get along well) but the daughter is unusually **shy** and **coy.**

Don't be **shy**.

Don't be <u>ashamed of</u> yourself when you make a mistake speaking English.

What a shame! It was a terribly shameful/disgraceful experience.

63) Dreamy

The girl is such a *dreamer*. She is obsessed with a Hollywood actor.

He is so ***dreamy***, she says about him.

Teenage girls have lots of pipedreams. They tend to imagine that they will be swept away by a knight in shining armour. 'Be realistic'. 'Come on, get real'. 'Wake up to yourself'.

These days, contrary to our expectations, girls are the ones who pick up the boys.

[cf. Pick up has several meanings. I need to pick up my English. The economy is picking up. I will pick you up. Please pick me up at seven].

64) Sissy

The boy is a ***sissy***. He cries like a girl.

The other kids laughed at him and called him a ***sissy*** because he didn't like sports.

The candidate touts his wartime service as evidence that he is not a **sissy**.

65) Cheeky

The baby is getting ***cheeky***.

You are a ***cheeky*** boy. Look at that ***cheeky*** face. Are you playing a game with me?

Such a ***cheeky*** boy!

66) Rowdy

I have ***rowdy*** neighbours. They are very *noisy*.

In Australia, you can usually make a big noise when you have a party at the weekend.

Other than the weekend, you've got to be careful, you need to have a chat with your neighbours beforehand. Otherwise, they will report you to the police.

- If you come across North Korean spies, please tip off the police. Please report this to the police.

- Other than that/apart from that, everything is ok for me.

Positive

67)   Chatty

My wife is quite *chatty* and talkative.

She is a very *chatty* person.

Can I *have a chat* with you? Can I have a word with you?

Let's have *a chit chat* at the weekend.

He is usually quiet but when it comes down to *footy* games, he becomes very *chatty*.

68)   Bubbly

We were greeted by two very *bubbly* members of check-in staff working on the counter.

The people we see are nearly always *bubbly*, and *giggly*.

My husband is usually very quiet but *when it comes to* political issues he becomes very *bubbly*.

69)   Tidy

My husband's personality is totally the opposite of mine. He is a *tidy and orderly* type of person but I am very laidback and *untidy*.

The wheelie bins look quite *tidy* along the lanes.

He has **a** *tidy* appearance because he refrains from drinking alcohol.

The house is in *a tidy* condition for the next occupant.

70)   Funny

The American is so *funky*. The clothes he wears, the way he acts and speaks is so *funny*.

I watched a comedy yesterday. It was so *funny*.

It was a *funny* story.

Believe me. After you graduate there will be so many girls for dating. It is not *funny*.

Funnily enough, he denies his mistakes.

It is so *funny* and I was cracking up so much It felt like my *tummy* was about to burst.

- You crack me up. I have a *tummy* ache. My *tummy* is aching.

71)   Customary

It is very *ordinary/normal* that children bow to their parents during New Year's holiday or Thanksgiving Day.

That's the *usual* condition.

It is **customary** that he acts like that. It is customary behavior.

This area has been left deliberately blank for you to make notes or add other words.

Notes for Ab/normality

3.2.5. Un/determined (Tenacity)

Positive

72) Steady

He studies very *steadily*. He is so <u>serious and studious</u>.

He is *steady* and stable.

- This will serve him in good stead in the long run.
- Learning to use a computer will serve you in good stead.
- Boys tend to be less tenacious than girls. They cannot keep their bums on their seats. They are easily distracted.

The couple has a *steady* relationship.

Now I have a *steady* job.

There is a *steady* table in the house.

Negative

73) Scatty

<u>Pay attention to</u> the ball when you play tennis.

You <u>make the same mistakes</u>.

You are so *scatty*. You are thoughtless.

In general, girls are more <u>tenacious</u> than boys. That is why girls usually excel over boys.

Boys tend to be *scatty*. They don't care much. They don't <u>concentrate on</u> their work much.

74) Silly

That's *bloody* (extremely) stupid and *silly*.

Your behaviour is *silly*. Don't be a *silly billy*. He is a *silly* boy.

You are behaving in a slightly *silly* way today.

75) Lazy

He is so *lazy*. He watches videos to <u>kill time</u> instead of studying.

He is **a *lazy*** bum**. He is so <u>slack</u> these days. Your work is so <u>slack.</u>

- You have arrived so early. You are *an early bird*.

- There is an old proverb that says an *early bird* catches the worm.

- *Early bird* registrations for the conference can get discounts.

- The *earlier* the better.

- First come first served. I have been <u>slack</u> lately.

- It is <u>such a fluke</u> that he won the lotto.

- He passed the most competitive exam. <u>What a fluke!</u>

- It was <u>just a fluke</u> to have received such a highly contested scholarship.

- It is an unexpected windfall. It is such a <u>fluke</u>.

- They are determined to show that their last win was <u>no fluke</u>.

76) Tardy

You will be courteous if you leave room for someone who might be just a bit ***tardy*** because of traffic.

Generally speaking, people are ***tardy***/slow to act in paying their bills.

77) Lousy

You are so ***lousy*** and **sloppy.** You need to <u>pull your weight</u> more.

He is a ***lousy*** player.

He is a ***lousy*** manager, because he did not reply to my emails.

This is a ***lousy*** piece of work.

This is ***lousy*** weather.

Even if the proposal contains ***lousy*** strategies, I am going to read it.

78) Sloppy

My daughter is so *lazy* and ***sloppy***. However, my son is a <u>hard worker.</u>

Young people's English is a bit ***sloppy***. He did a ***sloppy*** job.He said: "the players have to know that I will not stand for things being too ***sloppy*** for too long.

This area has been left deliberately blank for you to make notes or add other words.

Notes for Tenacity

Unit 3.3. APPRECIATION

3.3.1. Un/appealing (Reaction)

It is concerned with whether people **like or dislike something** and whether **things grab people's attention or not.** Reaction can refer to **people and things or facts.**

To describe people's appearance

1)   Shabby

She wears *shabby* old jeans. She is poorly dressed.

The old man looks *shabby* and s*cruffy.*

You look very *shabby* today.

2)   Bushy

I had my hair cut today, because my hair was so *bushy*.

I have become *bushy* of eyebrow, grey of hair, dry of skin, plump of middle.

You have a *bushy* beard.

3)   Spiky

After I got my hair cut, I realised that my hair style was too *spiky.*

I don't feel comfortable with that.

He was quite tall and buff and had *spiky* brown hair.

The thorn trees look suitably *spiky* and you certainly know not to land on them if you can help it.

4)   Cutey

The baby looks so *cute.* You are such a *cutey*. He is gorgeous. He is a good looking guy.

Look at the little girl. She looks like a doll.

She is very nice, but she's not afraid to *get cute* when there's something that she wants.

An example of a *cutey* is a charming little girl in pigtails with whom everyone is delighted.

5)   Chubby

I feed him very well. His face looks so ***chubby***. The baby is <u>plump</u>.

Move your ass, *fatty*.

Don't eat too much *fatty* food.

Look at the fat lady! Her arms are so *flabby*.

6)   Skinny

You have become so ***skinny***. You are so <u>slim</u>. Look at your ***boney*** arms!

I enrolled at a gym/fitness club/sports centre last year.

Since then, I have been exercising very hard to make myself fit and *healthy*.

Don't do too much exercise. Like taking drugs, exercising is also addictive. You have become a <u>gym junkie</u>.

7)   Muscley

My favourite movie star is Song Il-Guk. He looks so cool, and so handsome. He is also so ***muscley***/muscular.

8)   Manly

He can look so ***manly*** when he lifts heavy stuff. I have never been drawn to a movie star like him.

The female singer has a ***manly*** voice.

The male singer sang a *girly* song.

9)   Sporty

He is ***sporty***. He likes all types of sports.

He is so big and *mighty*. He has a big build.

10)   Perky

Look at the model. She is so hot and *steamy*. She is so vigorous and ***perky***. Her nipples are ***perky***.

My husband is already <u>out of steam</u>.

He used to be full of steam. He is not strong any more. <u>He is over the hill</u>.

Reaction is also used for **assessing things, processes and entities.**

This can be divided into several subcomponents.

Describing food

11)   Greasy

Chinese food is usually very *oily* and ***greasy,*** <u>whereas</u> Japanese food is simple, mild, bland and less *spicy*.

12)   Chilly

Korean food is usually very hot and *spicy,* because it has lots of chillies in it.

The food is too *salty*.

[cf. The weather gets <u>crisp</u> and ***chilly*** in autumn.]

In Autumn, when it gets cold, the weather feels ***chilly*** and crisp.

13)   Sugary

The food is too ***sugary****/*sweet.

Oils, crisps, sausages, pastries, fried foods (fatty foods), and sweets, cakes, chocolate and biscuits are all examples of *fatty* and ***sugary*** foods.

14)   Tangy

Mustard is ***tangy***.

The Indian food has a ***tangy*** taste and flavour, a bit like rocket.

15)   Crunchy

I love potato chips because they are ***crunchy*** and *crispy.*

[cf. He is very lazy but when it comes to <u>crunch time</u> he performs very well].

The cabbage should be slightly *crunchy*, not soft.

Add the spring onions and remove the pan from the heat so that they remain *crunchy*.

16) Junky/Junkie

Heroin *junkies* are wasting their lives.

That's all <u>junk</u> food and rubbish.

17) Chewy

The meat is not tender/soft and it is very *chewy*.

The Chinese cabbage is very *watery* because it is out of season. Korean people like *watery* soup.

The cooled caramels will be soft and *chewy* at this temperature.

When mixed with eggs, they create a soft custard base with *chewy* lemon pieces and a pleasantly bitter edge.

18) Yummy

My wife is a good cook. Look at the food she cooked.

Yum, beautiful. It is so *yummy*. I am already <u>drooling</u>. <u>Stop drooling</u>.

Serve over *fluffy* rice to soak up every last drop of the *yummy* sauce.

Almonds and cinnamon make this chocolaty beverage *yummy*.

Unsweetened coconut and *yummy* spices make this curry truly fulfilling.

I love Korean barbecue. It is really *tasty*.

- Can you give me some tips on how to cook?
- The secret is that you need to marinate with the right seasoning.
- Your seasoning is just right. I am good at seasoning.
- While I am good at cooking, I am poor at hiking.

19) Yucky

Korean food is very *yummy* but that soya bean paste is still too *smelly* and *yucky* for me.

While the food is delicious to you, it is <u>tasteless</u> to me*.The water was *dirty* and smelled *yucky.* I felt *yucky* after eating all that cake.

[Grammar 9: Concession (While, although, even if, even though, despite, in spite of, nevertheless, albeit) (ENGAGEMENT: Countering)]

- <u>While</u> I am willing to help (Positive +), I do not have much time available (Negative -).
- <u>Although/even though/even if</u> he worked hard (+), he failed in the exam (-).
- <u>Albeit</u> he worked hard, he failed in the exam.
- **Despite** his working hard, he failed in the exam.
- **In spite of** his working hard, he failed in the exam.
- **Despite the fact that** he worked hard, he failed in the exam.
- He worked hard, <u>but</u> he failed in the exam.
- He worked hard. <u>However</u>, he failed in the exam.
- He worked hard. <u>Nevertheless</u>, he failed in the exam.

Albeit is often used to introduce an adjectival or adverbial <u>phrase</u> that makes a concession about the preceding <u>noun</u> or <u>verb</u>. For example:

- His speech was impressive, <u>albeit</u> rather short.
- She appeared on the show, <u>albeit</u> briefly.
- It was an amazing computer, <u>albeit</u> expensive.
- The lesson was interesting, <u>albeit</u> difficult.

20) Tasty

The food you cook is really *tasty*.

Tundra cabbage is surprisingly *tasty* and tender for an over-wintered cabbage.

I don't *have access to* *my server as I use shared hosting, but robot cop sounds very *tasty*.

[Grammar 10: Transitive verbs]

Access (verb/noun), get access to.

- If you **have access to** the internet, you can gain useful information from it.
- Drag the icon to the desktop for easy access (noun).
- This is partly due to the lack of direct access (noun) from ward pcs to the hospital pharmacy.
- However I have been unable to access (verb) the basic setup screen to configure the gateway to access (verb) the internet.

21) Sticky

Australians don't seem to like *sticky* rice cake.

This is a *sticky* situation means that this is a difficult or unpleasant situation.

I have *sticky* fingers.

The room has *sticky* surfaces.

22) Savoury/Savory

The food is so *savoury*. I think the main distinction is just between sweet and *savory*, and sometimes people use the terms loosely.

A *savory* food can also be *salty* or *spicy*, but generally a sweet food isn't and just leans toward the *sugary* side. I think a *savory* food usually has some "flavour" though, *as opposed to* simply leaving the sugar out of something.

Compared with *Korean food, Australian food is less *salty*.

[Grammar 11: Comparison (ATTITUDE: APPRECIATION)]
'Compared to' and 'Compared with'

Both prepositions, **to** and **with**, can be used following **compare**. Neither is more correct than the other, but a slight distinction can be made in meaning. Firstly, **Compared To** has traditionally been preferred when the similarity between two things is the point of the comparison. On the other hand, **With** suggests that the differences between two things are as important as, if not more important than, the similarities.

- Life has been **compared to** a pilgrimage, **to** a drama, **to** a battle.

- Paris has been **compared to** ancient Athens.

- Congress may be **compared with** the British Parliament.

- Paris may be **compared with** modern London.

- I hesitate to compare my own works **to** those of someone like Dickens.

- We compared the facilities available **to** most city-dwellers with those available to people living in the country.

Secondly, while '**with**' is used for generalisations, '**to**' is used to compare statistical facts:

- A four-by-four uses more fuel **compared to** a mini.

- Compared *with* the Victorians, we are a much healthier society.

- **Compared with** Australia, China is much cheaper when it comes to commodity prices.

- **Compared to** South Korea, Australia is 50 times larger in terms of its size.

- For example, if you're graduating from high school you can go straight to college, **as opposed to** taking a year out of school and working.

23) Juicy

The fruit is so *juicy*. It is <u>succulent.</u>

We had *juicy*, delicate king fish with a good coating of subtle native spices.

The only rule is not to add wet ingredients, such as tomatoes, which are too *juicy*, otherwise the pizza becomes *soggy*.

We had *juicy* gossip about one of the contestants, Michelle.

24) Slimy/Slimey

The eels are very **slimy**.

I hate eating raw octopus. It is too **slimy**.

If you pick some of it out of the water, you will notice that it has a slightly **slimy** feel.

Toads are not **slimy** or *warty* and do not jump like frogs.

The sea creature was huge, *hairy*, and very **slimy**.

25) Soggy

If you put tomatoes in a sandwich, it gets **soggy** and *sloppy*. I don't like it.

Take care to clear up all the shattered pieces – they become very **soggy** on melting.

Soggy soil is a clever ecological solution for shade lovers.

In the living room the curtains smell like birds' poo and are all **soggy** and wet.

Describing places such as rooms & houses

26) Dusty

Your room is so *dirty*. The windows are so **dusty**. Look at the dust on the furniture.

27) Messy

Your room is so **messy**. It <u>stinks</u>. It is *stinky*.

It is <u>gross</u> and repulsive. Please *tidy up* your room.

Does the presence of customers make the shop look **messy**?

She has *messy* handwriting.

They have been through a *messy* divorce.

28)   Filthy

The <u>shanty towns</u> are very *filthy* and *dirty*.

When you travel by train, you can see that <u>stacks of</u> rubbish are <u>littered around</u> the railway.

It is <u>an eyesore</u>. Your room is so *dirty* and *untidy*.

Every time I see your room, I <u>frown.</u>

Your hands are *filthy*. Go and wash them immediately!

29)   Grotty

The rubbish bin is *grotty* and *smelly*.

Redfern is a *grotty* part of Sydney.

Lack of sleep not only makes you feel *grotty*, it <u>leads to</u> a suppression of the immune system.

From the outside, the upper floors looked fairly *grotty* but the ground floor was quite grand.

It is a standard hospital, quality-cheap and basic according to some, pretty *grotty* according to others.

30)   Smelly

Your room is *smelly* because your carpet is so old. It is so *musty*.

That is <u>gross</u> and disgusting.

Yuck. Your feet are *smelly* and <u>gross</u>.

Get the job done very quickly and the tray doesn't get **smelly**.

31)   Musty

Houses in Australia are very dark. They are *musty* and <u>damp.</u>

It is very damp and humid especially during the *rainy* season. Many houses get moldy because of the humidity.

Inside we found a slightly *musty* pub with walls covered with beer mats.

Don't feed hay which is *dusty*, or smells ***musty***.

The straw should smell sweet, not ***musty*** or stale.

32) Murky

The water in the swimming pool will get ***murky*** if you do not put chemicals in during the summer.

The afternoon was *cloudy* with a slight shower later and became ***murky*** toward evening.

With all these hidden cards, things can get pretty ***murky.***

Today was very ***murky***. I was surprised the picture came out at all.

33) Muggy

What is the weather like in Korea? Korea has four distinct seasons. The summer is very hot, humid and *sticky*. The summer is *rainy* when we have the rainy season. In summer, the weather is so <u>damp</u>.

It is a bit ***muggy*** outside.

Describing places and movies

34) Creepy

The movie is a bit ***creepy.***

The big doll looks ***creepy***.

I heard some strange noises. It was pretty ***creepy.***

Despite the weak ending, there are some genuinely ***creepy*** moments in the film.

This would be enough to make anyone feel ***creepy***.

35) Seedy

The street is <u>eerie</u> because it has many ***seedy*** bars.

Most people on the ***seedy*** street look under the influence of drugs.

Either way, it's a very ***seedy*** way of marketing.

We eventually found the place which turned out to be a rather ***seedy*** looking underground car park.

36) Spooky

The movie is *spooky.*

The strange man lives in a *spooky* and *eerie* old house.

My mum used to tell me *spooky* stories at bedtime.

While the sound is fuller, the effect is to make the lyrics even more *spooky*.

37) Gory

Spartacus is a *gory* movie. It involves* a lot of blood and violence.

I do not like these types of movies.

It's brutal in places, *gory* in places, and supernaturally *creepy* in places.

Perhaps a little too *gory* was the inclusion of a bowl of human ashes in the exhibits.

The movie contains lots of violence and *gory* scenes.

[Grammar 12: Transitive verbs: involve]

- I **was involved in** the court case.

- Change management **involves** planning, implementing and evaluating changes in an organization.

- Many people **are involved in** the incident.

- The scope of this position may **involve** some evening and weekend hours.

- I did not want to **involve** him in what we were talking about.

- Many university students **are engaged in** part-time work.

- Many university students **engage in** part-time jobs.

Describing weather

38) Foggy

On our way to the mountains, it was freezing cold. It was so *foggy* and *misty*, we could not drive.

My memory is a bit *foggy*.

In the morning, it gets *frosty*.

It is likely to be *stormy*. We had a *stormy* discussion.

It is too *foggy* in front of me, I cannot drive.

When a bushfire occurs, all the cities become *smoggy*.

The sky in Hong Kong is always *hazy*.

The room is very *smoky* because many people smoke cigarettes inside.

39) Nippy

It is a bit *nippy* today, because of the strong wind.

[cf. look at the *nippy* little sports car. The car moves very quickly and easily.]

40) Windy

Today is very *windy*. It is very *windy* today (cf. The street is windy, not straight).

41) Snowy

I love to go to a *snowy* mountain.

The winter here is not as *snowy* and *icy* as South Korea. However, you feel *much colder* than in South Korea.

42) Sunny

When it is **sunny**, it gets warm.

When it is *cloudy*, it gets cold. The sky is overcast today so it feels much colder.

Describing colour

43) Greeny/greenish

Bluey/pinky/yellowy colour.

Describing landscape

44) Slippery

The road is also **slippery** too.

When the floor gets wet, it becomes so **slippery**.

When you walk into a swamp, it is so *muddy*.

45) Hilly

This street is very **hilly**.

He lives in a **hilly** suburb.

46) Stony

This mountain is very **stony**. It has **a stony** hill.

Describing other things/clothes/furniture

Positive

47) Cuddly

The teddy bear doll is so *snuggly* and **cuddly**.

This blanket makes me feel *snuggly*.

Give me a **cuddle**/hug.

Give me a big hug.

48) Cosy

Your house is so *cosy,* like the house in the story of Snow White and the 7 dwarfs.

I like a *cosy* room.

49) Fancy

Your car looks so nice. It looks so *fancy*.

North Sydney is a <u>posh</u> area.

People living in that area are so *classy* and <u>posh</u>. They buy *fancy* furniture.

- You are too extravagant given your income.

- Your home is too luxurious considering* your income.

- Provided* that you have enough income, you can buy a house now.

- When you buy a house, you need to make allowance for/take into account/take into consideration your ability to repay.

[Grammar 13: Allowance (ENGAGEMENT) - Considering, make allowance, given that, etc.]

'Given the fact' implies it is proven, it is verifiable.

'Given that' means when you consider the following...

- I gave her a promotion **given the fact** that she is a good employee.

- It was surprising the government was re-elected, **given that** they had raised taxes so much.

- **Given/considering** his age, he is remarkably active.

- **Given/considering** her interest in children, teaching seems the right job for her.

[Grammar 14: Condition) - provided and providing: ENGAGEMENT]

The words provided and providing are interchangeable when used to mean 'on condition that'.

Examples:

- **Provided that** the weather is fine, we'll have a picnic on Saturday.

- **Providing that** the weather is fine, we'll have a picnic on Saturday.

- Tony will attend **provided that** Sarah is not chairing the meeting.

- The newspaper did not publish the photographs because they were given by a confidential source who gave them **provided that** we did not release them before the elections.

No Need for 'That': The word 'that' can be omitted.

Examples:

- **Provided** the weather is fine, we'll have a picnic on Saturday.

- **Providing** the weather is fine, we'll have a picnic on Saturday.

- You will be awarded a prize **on the condition** you complete the course.

- His reasoning is **based on the premise** that all people are equally capable of good and evil.

50) Lively

I love this city because the atmosphere is *lively*.

I enjoyed the *lively* rock concert.

The football match was *lively*.

51) Trendy

Designer brand bags are very *trendy*. They are <u>stylish and fashionable</u>.

They are currently very popular among young ladies. But I reckon it is just a *<u>passing fad</u>*.

Having a tattoo is *<u>just a passing fad</u>*.

He is a very <u>refined and cultured</u> person.

52) Fluffy

The cushion that I bought the other day is very *fluffy*.

I am an eight year old lady with a very *fluffy* tail!

I love rabbits too. They are so *fluffy* and loveable.

Negative

53) Flashy

In Thailand**,** every souvenir looks *flashy*.

I just want a good reliable car, nothing *flashy*.

He specializes in *flashy* technique, without much depth**.**

The actress was *flashily* dressed in the movie.

Evaluating people's appearance

54)   Tacky

You look very *tacky* when you wear these jeans.

They are <u>out of fashion</u> now.

When you buy *tacky* souvenirs, you will be bored with them within the week.

For me, Indian movies are a little loud and garish; quite *tacky*.

Some look great dressed up, others just look *tacky*.

55)   Crappy

What a bunch of *crap*.

This work is completely *crap*.

It is a *crappy* novel. It is full of rubbish.

Her jewellery looks very *crappy*.

56)   Saggy

After women undergo breast feeding, there is tendency for their breasts to become *saggy*.

Being exposed to the sun can make you old before your time – making your skin look *saggy*, *wrinkly* and *leathery*.

He is however a little *saggy* in this picture *due to** *it being* a hot day.

[Grammar 15: Causes and effects - Causative verbs (ENGAGEMENT)]. This is a very important grammar, particularly in writing.

- **Due to/because of** the rapid development of the internet, users can gain new knowledge conveniently.

- **Due to/because of the fact that** the internet has been developed rapidly, users can gain new knowledge conveniently.

- **Since/As/Now that** the internet has become prevalent, users can obtain updated information easily.

- The internet **enables** users **to** <u>access</u> new information easily.

- The internet **allows** users **to** <u>get access to</u> new information efficiently.

- The internet **helps** users **(to)** retrieve new information conveniently.

- This will **help (to) achieve** your goals.

- The internet **assists** students <u>in doing/to do</u> their assignments conveniently.

115

57)   Baggy

Your jeans are too *baggy*.

If *Baggy* packaging was not used on products then consumers would use little plastic baggies instead.

This fabric doesn't shrink, fade or go *baggy* even after frequent washing.

She always wears *baggy* clothes to hide her weight.

58)   Daggy

They look so **daggy**. They need to be <u>hemmed.</u>

The lovely Kim Wilkins says this: "Everything that made me *daggy* and unpopular has turned out to be a blessing", and I couldn't agree more.

Yet it is clear that despite our internal self-perception that the Anglican brand is *daggy*, the average Sydneysider is actually very warm towards us.

The *daggy* clothes you are wearing look uncool, unfashionable, but comfortable.

The boring, *daggy* lesbian is the one associated with difficult, challenging politics.

This area has been left deliberately blank for you to make notes or add other words.

Notes for Reaction

3.3.2. Un/balancing (Composition)

It is concerned with **whether or not something hangs together, is balanced or complicated**.

1)   Cruisy

His life is so smooth and *cruisy*. He just *cruises* around.

He sat for the most difficult exam, but he breezed through it.

I have to *sit for* the college entrance exam.

He inherited lots of property/real estate from his parents.

His parents *handed him down* a means to a good income.

He is so *lucky*, because his life will already **be a cruise**.

He has a *cruisy* job.

2)   Fiddly

It is quite *fiddly* closing this necklace because the latch is so small.

Cooking Korean food is very *fiddly* and elaborate.

I hate sewing because it is one of the most *fiddly* jobs.

Making jewellery is very *fiddly*.

Please stop fiddling with the computer when I am talking to you, pay attention to me.

I have fiddled around to work on this paper.

3)   Wordy

You need to be working on your paper more. *Tidy* it up a little bit and hand it in next week.

When you write an essay, don't make sentences too *flowery* and don't speak in *flowery* language. It becomes too **wordy** and *lengthy*.

Lecturers hate Asian students' digressive and indirect ways of writing essays.

Stop rambling and wandering around. Get down to the point first.

4) Corny

Corny is often used to describe someone or something that wants to be cool, but isn't. It sounds childish/lighthearted/a joke/*silly* not *funny*. For example, if your friend got a tattoo on his arm and thought it looked really cool, but you thought it looked stupid, you could say that the tattoo looked *corny*.

I know it sounds *corny* but it really was love at first sight.

It is a *corny* movie.

He makes a *corny* joke.

It may sound a little *corny*, but I like to visit places where few can go.

It is so *corny*, but it's very hard not to shed a tear.

Adam Sandler's movies are really *corny*.

My brother tries to talk with a British accent, but he sounds *corny* because he's not very good at it.

I bought these *corny* shoes yesterday for Halloween.

5) Cheesy

Cheesy is a similar word to *corny*. The difference between the two is that something that is *cheesy* is trying very hard to be cool. A *cheesy* person is someone who thinks he is the coolest person in the world, when in truth he's a dork.

It sounds *cheesy* (superficial), but I try to express myself.

It is an incredibly *cheesy* love song (of low quality and without style).

The film is long and somewhat *cheesy*, but it is very informative.

6) Fuzzy

This is a *fuzzy* area. My eyesight is getting *fuzzy* as I get older.

You can see a couple of rather *fuzzy* photographs of them here.

I feel uncomfortable and my vision goes *fuzzy* fairly quickly.

7)   Bulky

The parcel is so *heavy* and ***bulky*** that I cannot handle it by myself.

The bag is too ***bulky*** to carry with me at all times.

We have not had a chance to try one, but they do look a bit ***bulky*** and rugged.

It is difficult to flush away the ***bulky***, *greasy* stools.

8)   Hefty

He needs to diet, as he is too *heavy*. Look at the Yudo player. He is so strong, *heavy*, and muscular. He is ***hefty***.

I have made a ***hefty*** decision today.

You are so big. How much do you weigh? I am very *heavy*.

I dropped four dress sizes from what was a pretty ***hefty*** 16 down to a 10.

I have to pay ***hefty*** fines because I parked my car without a ticket.

In 1995 mobile phones were largely a business tool and still too ***hefty*** for the average pocket.

9)   Lofty

I will become a millionaire in two years' time. It sounds like a pretty ***lofty*** objective.

It is a ***lofty*** ambition. The house has ***lofty***/high ceilings.

It might be a tall order/demanding but could you finish the project by tomorrow?

10)   Chunky

The pieces are ***chunky***.

Give me a ***chunk*** of the meat.

Porcupines are slow movers with their ***chunky*** round bodies.

It's still early days for e-readers, and consumers can only choose between a few ***chunky***-looking models.

If you do not like ***chunky*** tomato sauce, you'll appreciate the *finely* diced carrots in this one.

11)   Roomy

The kitchen is so **roomy**. It is so spacious.

The interior of the car is **roomy**.

The house has **roomy** drawers, shelf, towel rail and bottle storage bin.

The underwater passage is quite **roomy**, about 3ft square.

12)   Scanty

Your literature review is **scanty** and insufficient.

You need to do more literature reviews.

Her clothing is very **scanty**.

She is wearing **scanty** panties.

You have to drink <u>plenty of</u> water if you want to keep yourself healthy <u>and fit.</u>

Can I give you more? No that's *plenty*.

This water reservoir used to have *plenty of* water. Now it <u>suffers from</u> a <u>lack of</u> water because of the drought.

We should use water <u>sparingly</u>. I would really *appreciate it* if you could <u>spare </u>some time for me.

13)   Foamy

This soap is very **foamy**.

A **foamy** bath can help dissolve the natural body greases.

Foamy waves swelled and gave off vapour.

14)   Glossy

The wooden floor boards look so *shiny* and **glossy**.

Vogue is a **glossy** magazine. It has lots of ads for high-end products.

He brought a **glossy** brochure for his presentation.

15)   Boggy

There are many reasons why a person may feel *boggy* (soft).

The house has *boggy* (soft and wet) ground.

The ground was *boggy* under foot.

16)   Flaky

Fish have lots of *flaky* scales.

These biscuits are very *flaky*.

They would twist and crack, and their surfaces would become *flaky*.

I have a *flaky*, *itchy* scalp.

17)   Prickly

This tree is very *prickly*.

When I tell a lie, it *pricks* my conscience.

When he <u>was falsely accused</u> because of my mistakes, my conscience *pricked*.

A cactus is very *prickly*.

I caught my foot on some rather *prickly* undergrowth which split the top of the boot.

She felt a *prick* as the thorn jabbed her foot.

He felt the *prick* of the needle.

18)   Thorny

Thorny shrubs <u>deter</u>* unwanted visitors <u>from</u> climbing over your fences.

The rose bush is very *thorny*.

It is a *thorny* issue, as it is a difficult topic for people to agree about.

This is proving to be a very *thorny* subject.

[Grammar 16: Negative causative verbs (ENGAGEMENT)]

- The goal is to **protect** healthy people **from** <u>developing</u> a disease or experiencing an injury in the first place.

- He should do more to **prevent** that **from** ever happening.

- They add that therapies designed to **prevent** this **from** happening during drug use could one day help to thwart chemical dependency.

- Procrastination severely **hinders** many people **from** putting their intentions into practice.

- Chewing gum may **stop** you **from** smoking heavily.

- Social Services and Health Commission services offer good support and help to **keep** people healthy and safe **from** abuse

19)   Wobbly

The leg of the chair is *wobbly*. It moves and is unstable.

I have a *wobbly* tooth and hate the thought of it dropping out.

I feel quite *wobbly*, having heard first hand from him.

My car has *wobbly* wheels and I need to fix them.

20)   Wonky

That painting hanging on the wall is *wonky*. You had better straighten it.

My face didn't go right back to normal, my smile is a little *wonky*, my eye seems a little smaller.

It is still important to get some good right angles or else the toy will still look *wonky*.

A w*onky* oak floor may lead to a furniture problem.

You have *wonky* teeth. They are <u>crooked not straight</u>. You have to get braces.

21)   Wiggly

Worms are *wiggly*.

Little children get restless if they have to sit still for a long time and they get **wiggly**.

Her bottom *wiggled* as she walked past.

He removed his shoes and *wiggled* his toes.

22)   Shaggy

My hair is too long and untidy. It is too *shaggy*. I need to have it cut.

The sheep dog has a *shaggy* coat of fur.

They had *shaggy*, thick wool and two horns.

My daughter has long untidy and *shaggy* hair.

23)   Shady

We went to find somewhere cool and *shady* to have a drink.

We have a big tree in our garden. So the garden is *shady*.

He is a *shady* and *dodgy* character.

24) Shadowy

Someone was waiting in the *shadowy* doorway.

It was very difficult to see him because he was standing in a *shadowy* corridor.

He is a *shadowy* figure. He is a bit suspicious.

25) Leafy

Most streets in Sydney are very green and *leafy*.

North Sydney is a *leafy* area.

This area has been left deliberately blank for you to make notes or add other words.

Notes for Composition

3.3.3. In/significant (Valuation)

1) Pricey

This stuff is very *pricey*.

House prices have become very <u>dear</u> and expensive lately.

I saw a wedding on the London Eye and it looked fantastic, it wasn't too *pricey* either.

Unfortunately, live telephone support can get *pricey* in a hurry.

I can tell you, furniture is quite *pricey* over here!

2) Costly

It is so *costly* to raise a child these days.

I have made a *costly* mistake. It is a very serious mistake that causes long-term damage.

Climate change is therefore likely to have considerable and potentially *costly* implications for the UK.

It is so *costly* to maintain the house.

The policy is *costly* to implement at a national level.

However, getting an eco-scheme wrong can be extremely *costly*.

It will be very *costly* once the ecosystem is destroyed by the pollution.

3) Rosy

Life is not *rosy* all the time. It has its <u>ups and downs.</u> Don't think that the world always revolves around you.

Oh dear, things don't look too *rosy* for us, do they?

No one should have the illusion that everything will all of a sudden become **rosy**.

She has *rosy* lips and cheeks that every man loves.

You know things aren't all *rosy* for these kids.

4) Easy-peasy

It is child's play. That is **easy-peasy**. It is <u>a piece of cake.</u>

Can you play "Mary had a little lamb on the piano"? Of course, that's **easy-peasy**!

*It is not easy** to* live in foreign countries. You may face many difficulties. Life is not *easy*, and it becomes complicated.

[Grammar 17: ATTITUDE (APPRECIATION)]

When valuing things, it is common to use the dummy subject or object 'it'. For example:

- **It is** extremely/vitally/crucially **important** for me **to** speak English fluently in order to get a decent job in Australia.

- **It is essential/integral/indispensable** for international students to have a good command of English to complete their studies in Australian Universities.

- I **find it** very important to speak fluent English in order to get a decent job in Australia.

Others include such evaluations as easy/difficult, un/necessary, im/possible, un/natural, etc. For example:

- **It is very difficult** for first year students to write an essay.

- First year students **find it difficult** to write an essay.

- Unless your soil is very sandy, **it is not necessary to** add organic material.

- **It is apparent/clear/evident** that oil reserves will be exhausted by 2050.

Negative

5)   Rusty

Your car is old. It is *rusty* all over. You need to dump it. Get rid of it.

When it comes to playing the piano, if you don't <u>polish</u> your skills, they get *rusty.*

I need to <u>brush up </u>on my English.

6)   Rocky

The mountain is *rocky* with cliffs and the sandy bays are in coves rather than long stretches.

A **rocky** shore is an intertidal area of seacoasts where solid rock predominates.

Our relationship is getting *shaky* and *rocky.* We have a *rocky* relationship.

Our marriage is <u>on the rocks</u> means our marriage is not strong.

How is he doing since he joined your church?

Oh he is <u>rock solid</u>. His faith is very firm and strong, because he is a devout Christian.

- You shouldn't <u>rock the boat now</u>, you need to be patient.

7)   Risky

It is too *risky* to buy stocks now. You <u>run the risk of </u>losing all your money.

<u>Strangely enough</u>, this is true, although it's a somewhat *risky* practice.

In addition, they are right to do so, since relying solely on Russian gas and fair business conduct appears too *risky.*

- When it comes to buying stocks, you've got to be very prudent/careful/circumspect, otherwise you will end up losing all your money.
- They ended up divorcing.
- At the end of the day, you have to face the music/face the consequences.
- We gave you good service. But at the end of the day, you started to pass the blame onto us.

8) Irony

It is such an **irony** that the ugly lady <u>is married to</u> a handsome man.

When she *married* him, he had no money. He <u>is married with three children</u>.

9) Faulty

The electric device is ***faulty***.

Everybody has faults/foibles, weak points and strong points.

The problem is you might have a ***faulty*** perception of a situation.

10) Leaky

Damage to blood vessels may cause inflammation, but may simply make blood vessels ***leaky***.

This tap is ***leaking***.

This gas pipe has rust everywhere. It can readily become ***leaky***.

The ***leaky*** roof is not being fixed by the council.

This area has been left deliberately blank for you to make notes or add other words.

Notes for Valuation

Section 4: Other expressions with Y

4.1. Common rhymes of abbreviations ending with Y

Y ending rhymes	Examples
Airy-fairy	He is an *airy-fairy* person. He is unrealistic. He has his head in the clouds. I've got my feet on the ground. While my husband has his head in the clouds, I am a down to earth person. '*Airy-fairy* bullshit' contrasts well with '*nitty–gritty*'
Argy-bargy	I am fed up with your *argy-bargy* way. It is too noisy and disruptive.
Hunky-dory	Everything will be *hunky-dory*. This means that everything will be fine.
Hurly-burly	The country is in a *hurly-burly* political situation
Hustle and bustle	City life has *hustle and bustle*.
Itsy bitsy or itty-bitty	I cannot explain the *itsy bitsy* details of the story now.
Lovey-dovey	I hate it when my mum and dad get all *lovey-dovey*. It is so embarrassing at their age.
Nitty-gritty	I have had enough of this superficial talk. Let's get down to the *nitty-gritty* of the issue. Let's get down to the *nitty-gritty* of the matter. The *nitty-gritty* of the problem is that he does not comply with the company rules.
Roly-poly	He is a really *roly-poly* guy, because he is very fat. The lollypop lady guides students to cross the road safely. Children like lollies.
Silly Billy	Don't be a *silly billy*.
Topsy-turvy	He went through *topsy-turvy* lifestyles.
Wishy-washy	Don't be so *wishy-washy*. Why can't you give me a definite answer?
Willy-nilly	Do not use your credit card *willy-nilly*. You should be careful. Hey! What are you doing with those seeds? You have to plant them in rows and evenly-spaced. Don't just toss them *willy-nilly!*

Other types of rhymes	Examples
Chit-chat	Let's have a **chit-chat** some other time. She is a very **chatty** person.
Claptrap	He talks a lot of claptrap and nonsense.
Chock- a-block	The bus was **chock-a-block**, I could not find a seat. The stadium was chock-a-block! It was a complete sell-out. You can imagine the atmosphere!
Knickknacks	The shop is decorated with many little **knickknacks**. I can't afford to buy anything but **knickknacks**.
Mishmash	Koreans like **mishmash** food. I like a **mishmash** of food. I have got a **mishmash** of an assignment.
Mumbo-jumbo	I think a lot of 'art talk' is **mumbo-jumbo**
Pitter-patter	The **pitter-patter** of little children running around a house. How long before I can hear the **pitter-patter** of little feet? Said by a pregnant woman to her obstetrician.
Riff- raff	They are **riff-raff** living in the slums.
Shipshape	Everything is **shipshape** in a Bristol fashion. My husband keeps things **shipshape**.
Tiptop	The house is in **tiptop** condition. You are now at the pinnacle of your life.
Tittle-tattle	I don't like office **tittle-tattle**. Women tend to engage in tittle-tattle gossip when they get together. **Chit-chat** relates to innocent gossip, while **tittle-tattle** relates to malicious gossip.
Tit-for-tat	The row was a **tit-for-tat** action.

4.2. Common abbreviations for nouns

Original words	Abbreviation (acronym)	Examples
Bad people	Baddies	
Barbeque	Barbie	
Bicycle	Bike	
Biscuit	Bikkie	
Breakfast	Brekky	
Bricklayer	Brickie	
Cat	Pussy	
Cigarette	Ciggies	
Dad	Daddy	
Dog	Doggy	
Electrician	Sparkie	
Football	Footy	
Good people and things	Goodies	
Grandmother	Granny	
Holiday	Hollies	
Hooligan	Hooly	
Husband	Hubby	
Mosquito	Mossie	
Mum	Mummy	
Nice person	Sweetie	
Old person	Oldie	
Politician	Pollie	
Sick leave	Sickie	
Soap operas	Soapies	
Surfboard rider	Surfie	
Television	Telly	
Umbrella	Brolly	
Underwear	Undies	
Vegetables	Veggies	
Woolworths	Woollies	

References

Bakhtin, M. (1981). *The Dialogic Imagination*. Austin TX: University of Texas Press.

Bakhtin, M. (1986). *Speech Genres and Other Late Essays*. Austin TX: University of Texas Press.

Bazerman, C. (n.d). Intertextualities: Volosinov, Bakhtin, Literary Theory, and Literacy Studies University of California, Santa Barbara. Retrieved from: http://education.ucsb.edu/bazerman/chapters/35.intertextualities.doc

Burns, D. D. (2008). *Feeling good together*. New York: Broadway books.

Butt, D., Fahey, R., Feez. S., Spinks, S. and Yallop, C. (2000). *Using Functional Grammar: An Explorer's Guide* (2nd ed.). Sydney: National Centre for English Language Teaching and Research.

Donaldson, R. M. (2011). Teaching foreign language conversation: A conversation norms approach. A Thesis California State University, Chico.

Eggins, S. (2000). *An introduction to systemic functional linguistics*. (2nd ed.). London: Continuum.

Farmer, F. (ed.) (1998) *Landmark essays on Bakhtin, rhetoric, and writing*. Mahwah, NJ: Lawrence Erlbaum.

Hall, J. K., G. Vitanova, and L. A. Marchenkova (eds.) (2005). *Dialogue with Bakhtin on second and foreign language learning: New perspectives*. Hillsdale, NJ: Lawrence Erlbaum.

Halliday, M. A. K. (1994). *An introduction to functional grammar*. London: Edward Arnold.

Halliday, M. A. K. & Matthiessen, C. (2004). *An introduction to functional grammar*. (3rd ed.). London: Edward Arnold.

Hammond, J. M., Macken-Horarik, M. (2001). Teachers' voices Teachers' practices, *Australian Journal of Language and Literacy*, 24 (2), 112-132.

Hood, S. (2004). Appraising research: Taking a stance in academic writing. Unpublished PhD thesis, University of Technology, Sydney, Australia.

Hood, S. (2010). Appraising research: Evaluation in academic writing. London: Palgrave Macmillan.

Jones, G & Polly, P. (2013). Scaffolding student learning by mastering the development of academic literacies through an oral assessment. In Coleman, k & Flood, a. (Eds). Marking time; Leading and managing the development of assessment in higher education, Champaign, Illinois: Common Grounds Publishing LLC.

Jones, P. & Chen, H. (2012). Teachers' knowledge about language: Issues of pedagogy and expertise. *Australian Journal of Language and Literacy*, 35 (2), 147-168.

Lee, S. H. (2006). The use of interpersonal resources in argumentative/ persuasive essay by tertiary students. Un published PhD thesis, University of Sydney, Australia.

Lee, S. H. (2007). An application of multiple coding for the analysis of ATTITUDE in an academic argument. *Journal of Linguistics and the Human Sciences*, 3(2), 165-190.

Lee, S. H. (2008a). The use of interpersonal resources in argumentative/ persuasive essays: Cross-cultural and grade-based differences between ESL and Australian tertiary students. VDM Verlag Dr Müller, Saarbrücken, Germany.

Lee, S. H. (2008b). An integrative framework for the analyses of argumentative/persuasive essays from an interpersonal perspective. *Journal of Text and Talk*, 28(2), pp. 239-270. DOI 10.1515/TEXT.2008.011

Lee, S. H. (2008c). Attitude in undergraduate persuasive essays. *Journal of Prospect*, 23(3), 43-58.

Lee, S. H. (2010a). Command strategy by balancing authority and respect by undergraduate students. *Journal of English for Academic Purposes*. 9(1), 61-75. doi:10.1016/j.jeap.2009.11.001

Lee, S. H. (2010b). Attribution in high-and low-graded persuasive essays by tertiary students. *Journal of Functions of Language*. 17(2), 181-206. DOI 1a 1075/fol.17.2.02lee.

Lee, S. H. (2010c). Differences in the use of Appraisal resources between L1 and L2 writers: Focusing on GRADUATION system. *Journal of Issues in Intercultural Communication ,*3 (1).21-47.

Lee, S. H. (2013). An evaluation on a team teaching by university students and lecturers in Australia. *Journal of Language Teaching and Research*, 4(5), 914-923. Doi: 10.4304/jltr.4.5.914-923.

Lee, S. H. (2014). Argumenta structure as an interactive resource by undergraduate students. *Journal of Linguistics and the Human Sciences,* 9(2), 273-299, doi: 10.1558/lhs.v9i2.273.

Lee, S. H. (in press). An extension of appraisal theory: Focusing on Valuation resources in persuasive essays. *Journal of Text and Talk.*

Macken-Horarik, M., & Martin, J. R. (Eds.) (2003). *Negotiating heteroglossia: Social perspectives on evaluation.* Text, 23(2).

Martin, J. R. (1984). Language, register, and genre. In F. Christie (ed.), *Children's Writing: Study Guide and Reader*. Geelong: Deakin University.

Martin, J. R. (2000). Beyond exchange: Appraisal systems in English, In S. Hunston and G. Thompson (eds.), *Evaluation in Text*. London: Oxford University Press, 142–175.

Martin, J. R., & Rose, D. (2003/2007). *Working with discourse. Meaning beyond the clause* (1st/2nd ed.). London and New York: Continuum.

Martin, J. R., & White, P. R. R. (2005/2007). *The Language of evaluation: Appraisal in English*. (1st/2nd ed.). London and New York: Palgrave/Macmillan.

Thompson, G. (2013). *Introducing functional grammar*. (3rd ed.). London & New York: Routledge.

White, P. (1998). *Telling Media Tales: The News Story as Rhetoric*. PhD thesis, University of Sydney.

White, P. (2004). Appraisal: an overview. Retrieved from:
http://www.grammatics.com/Appraisal/

Woodward-Kron, R. (2005) The role of genre and embedded genres in tertiary students' writing. Prospect, 20 (3), 24-41.

Write it Right (1996). *Exploring Literacy in School History*. NSW Department of School Education.

Further Help & Purchasing the Book

1) Author website: Help and advice can be found here:

- http://susanshin.wordpress.com

2) Publisher: You can find out where to get further copies of this book here:

- http://www.cranmorepublications.co.uk/y

3) Book stores in Australia:

- http://www.thenile.com.au/books
- http://www.coop.com.au
- http://www.booktopia.com.au
- http://www.fishpond.co.uk
- http://www.inbooks.com.au
- http://www.newsouthbooks.com.au
- http://www.palgravemacmillan.com.au

4) Espresso Book Machine:

- The Co-op Bookshop Custom Book Centre, Melbourne

5) US, UK, France, Germany, Italy, Spain, Canada:

- http://www.amazon.com
- http://www.amazon.co.uk
- http://www.amazon.fr

- http://www.amazon.de

- http://www.amazon.it

- http://www.amazon.es

- http://www.amazon.ca

6) Free worldwide delivery (including South Korea):

- http://www.bookdepository.com

7) Bulk Orders:

Discounts are available for orders over 20 copies. Please email cranmorepublications@gmail.com for details.

8) There is a companion book which is aimed at students rather than teachers:

Evaluating Words Ending with 'Y': Mastering 'Real' Everyday English

http://www.cranmorepublications.co.uk/student

9) Contact the author:

susanshin713@yahoo.com.au   or   sook09@hotmail.com

If you know of any other 'Y' expressions which could be included in the book, or if you have any comments or feedback, then it would be great to hear from you.

Thank you

✎ Test yourself!
Commonly used words that end in 'Y'

Please read through the following expressions containing commonly used words that end in 'Y' to see how many you know and use in everyday conversation. Simply tick the relevant column. If you tick less than 10 boxes in Column 1 then you need to consider buying this book.

	Column 1	Column 2	Column 3
	I know and use it in everyday conversation	I understand but I never use it	I don't know the expression
She is a very **bossy** woman.			
My neighbour tends to be **snobby.** They do not like to mix with people from other backgrounds.			
My 5-year-old boy is very **fussy.** He does not eat any vegetables.			
My husband is a very **finicky** person, while I am quite **laidback.**			
He's got a **quirky** sense of humour. Not everyone finds his jokes funny.			
Children usually get very **cranky** when they are not fed.			
He is very **grumpy** today for some reason.			
She is very **stingy.** She only gave me a card for my birthday.			
He is such a **jolly** guy.			
That mechanic is pretty **dodgy.**			
She is very **nasty.** So everyone hates her.			
He looks so **geeky** with those thick glasses he wears.			
There are all these **brainy** people at university.			
She usually wears **tacky** clothes.			
When the alarm bell rings, don't get all **panicky.**			
There are some pretty **freaky** people on Oxford Street on a Saturday night.			
It is very **fiddly** to make this kind of jewellery. You need very steady hands.			
Total			

How many boxes did you tick in Column 1?

1-5 (   )   6-10 (   )   11-15 (   )   More than 15 (   )

141

www.ingramcontent.com/pod-product-compliance
Lightning Source LLC
Chambersburg PA
CBHW081232090426
42738CB00016B/3265